Public sector reform

Public sector reform
Principles for improving the education system

Frank Coffield, Richard Steer, Rebecca Allen,
Anna Vignoles, Gemma Moss and Carol Vincent

Bedford Way Papers

First published in 2007 by the Institute of Education, University of London,
20 Bedford Way, London WC1H 0AL
www.ioe.ac.uk/publications

© Institute of Education, University of London 2007

British Library Cataloguing in Publication Data:
A catalogue record for this publication is available from the British Library

ISBN 978 0 85473 773 4

Design by River Design, Edinburgh
Typeset by Chapman Design Limited
Printed by dsicolourworks

Contents

Preface

The Prime Minister's Strategy Unit (PMSU) produced in 2006 a new model of reform for the public services which purports to create more radical change than anything seen so far. The research evidence for this model, however, is either weak, mixed or non-existent. It is a response to the problems that policy-makers now face after ten years of over-using one mechanism of change, namely, top-down management, which has alienated the professionals. It appears seductively simple because it ignores some of the main problems faced by practitioners.

We are a team of researchers from the Institute of Education, University of London, who wish to comment upon the likely impacts of this model on education, our area of expertise. We hope in this respect to enter into dialogue with policy-makers on the limitations of the current approaches to changing the system, and put forward some alternative principles which we think should underpin any further attempts at reform. The model, as proposed by PMSU, is made up of four main elements: top-down performance management; market incentives; choice and voice; and capability and capacity. We devote a chapter to each of these elements, exploring the research evidence for the claims made, and finding it wanting.

Chapter 3 examines the limitations of top-down performance management in relation to the national literacy and numeracy strategies. After some initial success, they have shown a much more modest influence on outcomes. Moreover, the pace of innovation, driven by the centre, has outstripped the capacity of schools to respond, while innovation has been valued over and above consistency and quality.

Chapter 4 reviews a very extensive literature on market incentives in schools and concludes that in the UK no causal connections have been established between, on the one hand, choice and competition, and, on the other, student attainment. There are also limitations to the application of market principles in education, and a pressing need for better safeguards against the selection of students by schools.

After reviewing the evidence, Chapter 5 concludes that choice and voice, as presented by PMSU, are not strong mechanisms for reform in education. The difficulties in fostering an individual or a collective voice for parents, or in reconciling conflicting voices, have not been recognised by the PMSU team. We argue, however, that voice has great potential as a lever of change.

Chapter 6 argues that, although the government is making substantial investments to improve the capacity of the workforce, if it is now to treat staff as essential partners, it must create feedback loops to enable professionals to explain to policy-makers the strengths and weaknesses of policy and to be engaged in redesigning it. The government's model of leadership will also have to change because the current version is focused on faithfully carrying out whatever reforms the government stipulates.

We decided against producing an alternative model of our own because the world of professional practice and the task of improving it on a national scale are much more complicated than this model, or any model, would suggest. Instead, we draw attention to three problems and set out three principles of procedure.

First, there needs to be wider acknowledgement of the complexities involved in changing the education system. For example, the main factors which interact with each other in classrooms include: curriculum, pedagogy, management, abilities of students, expertise of teachers, resources, technology, national policies on assessment, socio-economic influences, and so on.

Second, an historical examination of why schools have changed reforms rather than reforms changing schools points to barriers to change created by 'the grammar of schooling'. By this phrase is meant such organisational regularities as the division of knowledge into different subjects which shape the ways in which teachers work. Plans for reform need to understand schools as complex, social institutions with their own cultures.

Third, we need a more sophisticated notion of what will be required to create a 'self-improving system'. Radical and enduring change requires depth (altering teachers' beliefs and practices), sustainability (change which lasts), spread (of reform principles from classrooms to school policies) and a shift in the ownership of reforms (to teachers, schools and local authorities).

We end by arguing for three principles for improving the quality of learning. We need to give up the macho talk of 'step changes' and instead introduce a more moderate pace of change. The timescales of politicians and professionals are at variance; and schools need continuity and stability as well as change.

This high point of centralisation has probably passed, but the new talk of decentralisation has still to be turned into changed behaviour by ministers. There needs to be a more equal sharing of power between policy-makers and professionals, between teachers and parents, and between teachers and students. Reforms need to be both 'tight' (with close adherence to core principles) and 'loose' (adapted to local conditions).

If the core business of education is improving the quality of teaching and learning, then most attention should be devoted to the relationship between tutors and students. Too much of the time and energy of teachers and head teachers is being diverted to meeting targets, responding to initiatives and maximising funding and away from sustained, collaborative learning with colleagues.

Finally, we conclude that, while the professional empowerment of teachers is a necessary condition of success, it is not a sufficient condition. Teachers need to be given more scope for creativity and engagement in policy, but at the same time they need to be held accountable for the decisions they make.

Frank Coffield

Abbreviations

DfES   Department for Education and Skills
FE   Further education
HEI   Higher education institutions
HMIE   HM Inspectorate of Education
LAs   Local authorities
LLUK   Lifelong Learning UK
NICE   National Institute of Health and Clinical Excellence
NLS   National Literacy Strategy
PIRLS   Progress in International Reading Literacy Study
PISA   Programme for International Student Assessment
PMSU   The Prime Minister's Strategy Unit
PNS   Primary National Strategy
PSA   Public Service Agreement
PTA   Parent Teacher Association

Notes on contributors

Frank Coffield is Professor of Education at the Institute of Education, University of London, having previously worked in the Universities of Newcastle, Durham and Keele. Earlier, he taught in a comprehensive school, an approved school and Jordanhill College of Education in Scotland. He was Director of the ESRC's research programme into The Learning Society from 1994 to 2000, and edited four reports and two volumes of findings from the programme.

In 2004 he published *Learning Styles and Pedagogy in Post-16 Learning: A Systematic and Critical Review* and *Should we be Using Learning Styles: What Research has to Say to Practice*. Both are downloadable free of charge from: www.lsda.org.uk/pubs/dbaseout/download.asp? code=1540 and code=1543.

He is currently the Principal Investigator of an ESRC project in the Teaching and Learning Programme, entitled 'The Impact of Policy on Learning and Inclusion in the New Learning and Skills Sector'. A book, *Improving Learning, Skills and Inclusion: The Impact of Policy on Post-Compulsory Education* is to be published by RoutledgeFalmer. His inaugural lecture entitled 'Running Ever Faster Down the Wrong Road: An alternative future for Education and Skills' is available from the Institute of Education, London.

Richard Steer is a Research Officer at the Institute of Education, University of London. He has been at the Institute for three years, working on an ESRC Teaching and Learning Research Programme project looking at 'The Impact of Policy on Learning and Inclusion in the New Learning and Skills Sector'. His main interests are in post-compulsory education and training policies, governance and social inclusion. Richard has previously carried out research and evaluation on community-based interventions to help young people who are NEET (not in education, employment or training) whilst working at the Community Development Foundation.

Rebecca Allen is a PhD student in the Centre for Economics of Education, Institute of Education. Her thesis is entitled 'Choice-based secondary school admissions in England: social stratification and the distribution of educational outcomes'. Her work uses national pupil administrative datasets to explore current levels of pupil sorting and how this impacts on school performance. Before returning to full-time study, Becky was a secondary school economics teacher in a London comprehensive.

Anna Vignoles is a Reader in the Economics of Education at the Institute of Education, University of London. Her research interests include issues pertaining to equity in education, school choice, markets in education and the economic value of schooling. She is an adviser to both HM Treasury and the Sector Skills Development Agency, and has undertaken extensive research for the Department for Education and Skills. Recently, she has provided advice to the House of Commons Education and Skills Committee investigation of higher education funding, the House of Lords Economic Affairs Select Committee, as part of their inquiry into education and training opportunities for young people, as well as to Lord Leitch's Review of Skills.

Gemma Moss is Reader in Education at the Institute of Education, University of London. She specialises in the study of literacy policy, gender and literacy, and children's informal literacy practices and their relationship to the school curriculum. She has held a succession of research grants from the ESRC on these topics. She has also recently co-directed an evaluation of the use of IWBs in London secondary schools on behalf of the DfES. Her most recent book, *Literacy and Gender: Researching Texts, Contexts and Readers*, is published by RoutledgeFalmer.

Carol Vincent is a Reader in Education at the Institute of Education,

University of London. Her research interests include social justice, social class, parents' relations with childcare and education providers, and markets in education and care, and she has written extensively on these topics. Her publications, written with Stephen Ball, include *Childcare, Choice and Class Practices* (Routledge, 2006).

1 Introduction

Richard Steer and Frank Coffield

The management of all our public services is undergoing radical change. The government has signalled the end of a decade of centralised control and top-down performance management, and is introducing a new approach that aims to transform public services into 'self-improving' systems. It is an ideal time to take stock. What, for example, have we learned from the attempts of New Labour over the last ten years to reform the public services? The Prime Minister's Strategy Unit (PMSU) produced in 2006 a new model of reform, which is ushering in a more radical phase of reform than anything we have experienced so far. But is the new model adequate to the task? Is it based on sound evidence? Does the model need to be amended slightly or fundamentally redesigned? Or do we need an alternative set of principles on which to base future reforms?

This book seeks to engage critically and constructively with this new model, which is already being applied across the public services. The role we have chosen to play is that of critical friends, with as much emphasis on the adjective as on the noun, and with the aim of improving not just policy but, far more importantly, outcomes for learners. We have decided to play to our strengths and so, although the model deals with all the public services such as health, social care, local government, the criminal justice system and so on, we will restrict ourselves to commenting upon education, which is our area of expertise. We will leave it to others to determine the extent to which our arguments apply to the other public services. The authors of this response are a team of academics and researchers from the Institute of Education, University of London.[1] We come from a variety of disciplinary backgrounds and specialise in different phases of education, bringing different perspectives to bear on the government's reform agenda. In our view the government's model has far-reaching implications for the education system and we wish to open up a public debate about whether these are the right reforms, or the right balance and combination of measures, to achieve the improvements we all desire. Our own view is that the model is more a response to the problems faced by policy-makers than to those faced by practitioners.

In March 2007, the government issued a further document, entitled *Building on progress: public services*, as part of its ambitious review of policy. The document considers 'what has worked (and what has not); what should be intensified; and what new directions should be pursued' (H M Government 2007: 78). Writing in the Foreword, the Prime Minister made clear that the government will not turn back and eschew further reform, but will 'continue with the underlying mission to personalise and to empower' (ibid.: 4).

The election of the New Labour government in 1997 marked a watershed for public services in the UK. Elected on a manifesto that promised that education would be 'our number one priority', and which committed the government to increasing the share of national income spent on education and health, the new administration delivered on its pledges to increase investment in public services (Labour Party Manifesto 1997). The UK government now spends an additional £10 billion a year on education and £20 billion more each year on the Health Service, compared to 1997 spending levels (PMSU 2006a: 18). The idea that increased investment in public services should be accompanied by 'modernising' reforms, promoting greater choice for service users and increased involvement of the private sector in public services, had become a firmly established principle by the start of Labour's second term of office in 2001.

The government first aired its model of public service reform in June 2006 through the publication of *The UK Government's Approach to*

Public Service Reform – A Discussion Paper (PMSU 2006a). Speaking at the conference '21st Century Public Services – Putting People First', where the PMSU discussion paper was launched, Tony Blair said: 'There is a basic deal here. Investment for results'. He argued that public support for increased investment in services would be jeopardised unless it could be shown 'demonstrably that the service has got radically better' (Blair 2006). 'Better Public Services for All' is the slogan at the centre of the model and this is its principal objective.

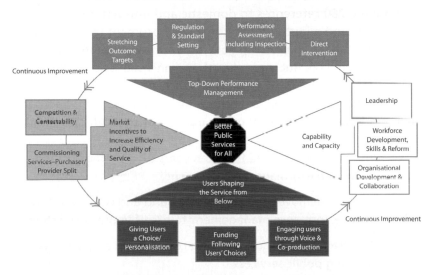

Figure 1 Government model of public service reform (PMSU 2006a: 8)

The main underpinning arguments behind the model are: that there have been major improvements across public services since 1997; that these improvements are the result of increased investment allied to a tough regime of top-down performance management; but that the limits of what can be achieved through top-down approaches have now been reached. The model (shown in Figure 1) seeks to create a new 'self-improving system' by counterbalancing top-down control with bottom-up pressure from 'users shaping the service from below' and horizontal pressures exerted through market incentives to increase efficiency and quality, and by improving the capability and capacity of the public sector workforce.

The publication of the PMSU discussion paper, openly setting out the government's framework for policy development, is to be applauded. We in reply are offering principled dissent and constructive feedback. It is also to be welcomed that the PMSU document has engaged with a wide spectrum of evidence in making the case for its model of public service reform. This has been done in considerable detail, as can be seen by the 280 references to domestic and international research, policy texts and ministerial speeches. The document recognises that each of the dimensions of the government model has its limitations and associated risks. But in our view these concessions do not go nearly far enough.

The PMSU discussion paper raises fundamental questions about the past and future management of our public services, such as:

- What has been learned from ten years of imposing a tough regime of performance management?

- How can we move beyond the command and control of top-down performance management to a 'self-improving system'?

- What are the limitations of using competition as a lever for improving public services?

- What other levers should be used?

There are further, difficult questions which we want to discuss. For example: How is poor performance best dealt with? Can we afford to leave reform to the professionals? Is the market the most efficient and equitable means of organising provision?

Any reforming government would pose such questions; it is the answers offered by the PMSU which give us cause for concern. We wish to congratulate the government on the successes it has had in raising standards and increasing levels of participation in education. However, the difficulties of reforming a system through constant top-down pressure are underplayed. On this point we would draw attention to the research literature which is ignored by the PMSU document, which describes the serious and well-known consequences of the audit culture which government policy has brought into being (e.g. Harlen and Deakin Crick 2002; Power 1994; Reay and Wiliam 1999; Ball 2003). Some of the perverse effects have been shown to be: a narrowing of the curriculum, teachers adopting a didactic style of teaching, and low-achieving students having their self-esteem lowered by repeated practice tests.

Similarly, the PMSU text is silent about persistent race inequalities (Gillborn and Youdell 2000) and about the latest evidence from the Equalities Review (2007: 24) which argues that, at the current rate of progress, we will never close the ethnic qualification gap.

Meanwhile, the positive impacts of the new types of pressure are correspondingly overestimated in the government's discussion paper. Crucially, there is no acknowledgement that the four types of pressure in the model conflict with each other in practice. To give just one example of this, many local Sure Start projects made considerable efforts to involve parents in determining and planning the types of services they wanted in their local area. However, this positive instance of 'users shaping the service from below' was overridden when centrally determined priorities changed and the government's focus shifted to expanding childcare places as part of a drive to encourage mothers back into work (Glass 2005). Bottom-up pressure from the 'users' was in conflict with the pursuit of top-down targets. There are plenty of other examples from the education sector, some of which will be highlighted in subsequent chapters.

The chapters have been written by different authors, and each engages with the reform model from a different angle, drawing upon the writers' expertise in different phases of education such as primary, secondary and the post-compulsory sector. Moreover, in this short book we do not attempt to cover all the issues raised by the PMSU document – such as the governance of schools, city academies and qualifications and assessment. What our different viewpoints have in common, however, is that each finds the government's approach to public service reform wanting in important respects. Taken together they give serious cause for concern about whether the new model of public service reform will work in education. The authors of each chapter end with suggestions for policy, which are then picked up in the final chapter.

Chapter 2 offers a brief summary of the new model of reform, discusses why it is thought necessary by government and describes the four main features of the model: top-down performance management; market incentives; choice and voice; and capability and capacity. It ends by arguing that there are ten implicit assumptions behind the model which need to be made explicit and which need to be challenged.

In Chapter 3, Gemma Moss explores the limitations of top-down performance management through the case of the government's National Literacy Strategy. While a top-down approach to standardising classroom practice brought about improvements in the first few years, results have subsequently been more modest. Moss argues that, while the government is right to question the long-term effectiveness of top-down approaches, there are deeper problems that need to be addressed: the distortion of key areas of professional practice through the politicisation of educational policy-making in England; and the valorisation of innovation above other virtues such as consistency or quality. In this respect, there are lessons that can be learned from approaches in Scotland.

Rebecca Allen and Anna Vignoles in Chapter 4 examine the PMSU's claims about the beneficial effects of school competition. They argue not only that these claims are founded on questionable theoretical assumptions, but that they are also based on a selective reading of the empirical evidence. Contrary to the case put forward in the PMSU discussion paper, there is no clear evidence that parents in the UK genuinely want school choice; the claim that choice can lead to more equitable outcomes is not supported by the evidence; and most research in the UK indicates that there is no overall effect of choice or competition on pupil performance.

In Chapter 5, Carol Vincent considers the concept of user voice in the

PMSU, looking specifically at parental voice in schools. The role of voice within the PMSU model is seriously underdeveloped, with hardly any acknowledgement of the difficulties and complexities inherent in supporting the meaningful exercise of parental voice. Nonetheless, voice has the potential to act as a significant lever for reform, if it were taken more seriously and recognised as being distinct from user choice.

In Chapter 6, Frank Coffield scrutinises the final element of the reform model, capability and capacity. While the government's rhetoric around its commitment to improving the 'calibre, skills, attitude and motivation' of the teaching workforce seeks to include professionals as partners in reform, there are worrying signs that the teaching profession is still regarded with distrust – as a barrier to progress rather than the main means of achieving it. Key omissions in the PMSU's argument are highlighted, such as: the failure to address long-standing inequalities between different parts of the education system; the absence of systemic feedback loops through which staff could inform policy development; and, perhaps most seriously of all, the lack of recognition that changing professional practice takes time and cannot be quickly and easily directed from on high.

The evidence and analysis presented in these chapters lead us to conclude that a different approach to reform is urgently needed, and in the final chapter we set out some principles to underpin such an approach. Our vision is of a genuine break from a pressure-driven and top-down system, which needs to be replaced by one that supports the improvement of teaching and learning through greater partnership and dialogue. This will require a more moderate pace of change, a rebalancing of power and relationships to harness the knowledge, creativity and energies of all partners, and a determination to place teaching and learning at the heart of the system.

Note
1 We wish to thank the Director and the Director of Research at the Institute of Education, University of London for the funding which made this project possible. We are also grateful to those colleagues who helped us to improve an earlier version of this book by discussing it at an internal seminar in June 2007.

2 The UK government's model of public service reform

Frank Coffield and Richard Steer

2.1 The origins of the public service reform model

Although the PMSU model is new, many of the ideas contained within it are well-established themes of the Labour government's three terms in office, in particular the idea that public services must continually 'modernise' in order to keep pace with technological change and rising expectations of modern service users. Furthermore, some of the central principles, such as the use of market incentives to improve the performance of public services, can be traced back to Conservative policies during the 1980s and 1990s (Newman 2000; Ball 2007). To some extent, then, the PMSU discussion paper represents an attempt to set out, explain and also legitimate a reform programme that was already well underway.

What is distinctively new about the model is the claimed shift in emphasis away from government assuming prime responsibility for regulating public services, in favour of an approach which seeks to create 'self-improving systems' through a *combination* of top-down, horizontal and bottom-up pressures. Whether this shift is taking place as the government claims, and whether it is capable of generating the radical improvements hoped for in education, are the subjects of the following chapters. But before we look in detail at the ramifications for education, it is necessary to first introduce the model. In this chapter we set out to answer the following three questions: Why is further public service reform thought to be necessary? What are the features of a 'self-improving system'? What assumptions underpin the government's reform model, and are they correct?

2.2 Why is public service reform thought to be necessary?

The PMSU discussion paper sets out the government's vision as being to ensure that 'everyone should have access to public services that are efficient, effective, excellent, equitable, empowering and constantly improving' (PMSU 2006a: 7). The need for a new approach to public service reform is linked to fundamental shifts in society which have significantly altered the context in which public services have to operate. These span social and demographic, economic and technological changes, which, combined with greater affluence and educational opportunity, have changed public attitudes towards – and expectations of – public services:

> Compared with half a century ago, people are accustomed to much greater control over their lives. And higher educational standards mean that they are better equipped to exercise choice, much less likely to settle for second best and less likely to accept government or 'expert' advice without question or to allow others to make choices and decisions on their behalf.
>
> (PMSU 2006a: 18)

Correspondingly, it is argued that citizens' expectations of public services have also increased.

In addition to these long-term trends, the PMSU discussion paper also presents a narrative about more recent changes in government and its approach to public services. This account begins in 1997 when New Labour came into office and was confronted with a need to increase investment in key public services, following 'years of under-investment' (ibid.: 21). However, this increased investment was 'accompanied by a tougher performance management regime which was intended to provide a clear and rapid signal that improved outputs were expected from the additional expenditure' (ibid.: 21). This tough new regime consisted of Public Service Agreement (PSA) targets, new regulatory approaches to ensure wider adoption of 'best practice', greater inspection of public services, and new powers of intervention where services are failing. This phase of increased investment allied to top-down performance management is credited with a range of improvements in key public services. It is claimed that in education the combined use of targets, regulation, performance assessment and direct intervention have contributed to the following achievements:

- The proportion of primary schools judged by Ofsted to be good or excellent has risen from 45% in 1997 to 74% in 2004/5, and among secondary schools during the same period the proportion of schools judged to be good or excellent rose from 59% to 78%;

- Following the introduction of Key Stage 3 strategies in 2001, the number of 14-year-olds achieving the target level for their age increased by 54,000 in English and by 48,000 in maths (compared with 2001);

- GCSE attainment has improved, with over 56% of 16-year-olds now achieving five A*–C grades, up from 45% in 1997 (with greater rates of improvement in inner London and in specialist schools);

- Between 1997 and 2005 the number of secondary schools in which fewer than 25% of pupils achieved five good GCSEs fell from 616 to 105; meanwhile, the number of non-selective schools in which at least 70% of pupils achieved five good GCSEs increased from 83 in 1997 to 515 in 2004/5 (PMSU 2006a: 39–40).

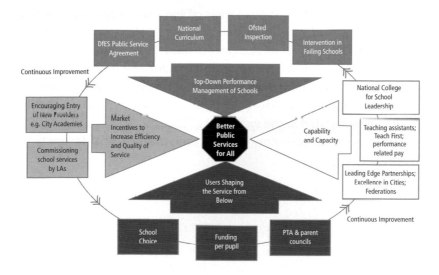

Figure 2 The dimensions of a self-improving system for schools
(PMSU 2006a: 25)

2.3 What are the features of a 'self-improving system'?

The government's model seeks to replace top-down pressure on public services with a more balanced set of mechanisms, combining pressure from above in the form of 'top-down performance management', horizontal pressures from 'market incentives to increase efficiency and quality of service' and improvements in the 'capability and capacity' of those delivering public services and, finally, 'users shaping the service from below'. These four types of pressure are for the first time brought together into one powerful model where the strengths of one form compensate for the weaknesses of another, and vice-versa. While these four elements or pressures are seen constituting the basic reform model, there will be 'variation within, as well as among, services in what combination of pressures is best at sustaining performance improvement' (PMSU 2006a: 25). The PMSU document shows this through different illustrative models of the particular pressures that are applicable to schools, hospitals and local policing. The particular adaptation of the public service reform model as it would apply in the schools sector, reproduced from the PMSU discussion paper, is shown in Figure 2. The model is deemed to be 'self-improving' 'because it is intended that incentives for continuous improvement and innovation should be embedded in the system itself' (ibid: 23).

A brief introduction is now given to each of the four different types of pressure.

(i) Top-down performance management

The PMSU discussion paper specifies four elements of top-down performance management:

- objectives, targets, and performance indicators, which set specific ambitions for improvement in priority areas of public service;

- regulation, including the setting of minimum service standards, which specifies the quantity, quality and type of service that users should receive;

- performance assessment, including inspection, to monitor and assess whether providers are meeting those standards;

- intervention to tackle failing or underperforming providers.

The use of these top-down measures since 1997, allied to increased investment in public services, is claimed to have led to the improvements listed above. It is, however, recognised that top-down performance management has its downsides. Those admitted in the document include that it can increase bureaucracy, stifle innovation and local initiative, create perverse incentives and de-motivate frontline professionals. These drawbacks are not considered insurmountable, but rather the elements of top-down performance management are to be 'designed in a way that maximises performance improvements and minimises the risks' (PMSU 2006a: 33).

To maximise the effectiveness of the levers used by top-down performance management, it is argued that: the particular combination of levers needs to be tailored to specific service areas; targets need to be reformed (e.g. by having fewer targets overall, simpler outcome-based targets rather than output measures, and decentralised target-setting); and the burden of regulation and performance assessment needs to be streamlined.

(ii) Market incentives

Market incentives refer to two main mechanisms: competition and contestability. Competition denotes any situation in which 'a range of providers continually compete with each other for the custom of individual users' (PMSU 2006a: 48). The concept of contestability, meanwhile, refers to 'widening the market to create more suppliers of public services', which, it is claimed, has the theoretical advantages of improving the quality of management, bringing about more choice through more providers, more choice because provision is higher quality, more innovation and better value for money (The Work Foundation 2005). The introduction of competition and contestability into the public services is based upon the view that those who work in the public services are motivated by a combination of altruistic and self-interested concerns and may act either as 'knights' or 'knaves'.

> The evidence is mixed about how far professionals, such as doctors and teachers, can be assumed to be only concerned about the interest of the people that they are serving.
>
> (PMSU 2006a: 59)

The conclusion arising from this is that

> a significant challenge for public service reform is the need to construct a system which motivates the most self-interested and also

gives knights the space and the encouragement to allow altruism to flourish.

(PMSU 2006a: 59)

Competition should be underpinned by new funding arrangements in which funding follows 'user choices, so successful providers are rewarded with extra revenues and encouraged to expand whilst unsuccessful providers are penalised' (ibid.: 52). The risks of a poorly designed system of competition and contestability are identified as being: commissioning may fail to attract new providers; there may be poor-quality provision if providers are not adequately held to account and/or there is insufficient competition between providers; high transaction costs on all sides in tendering for contracts; and the danger of undermining the ethos of public services.

The government's response to these potentially adverse effects of competition is to give itself the role of fostering collaboration between providers. Collaboration within a competitive system is not seen as a contradiction, but as providing opportunities for the sharing of costs between providers, pooling risks and promoting experimentation, speeding the diffusion of 'best practice', providing support for under-performing providers and improving access through more joined-up approaches. Recognising that 'there is clearly a risk that organisations may be deterred from undertaking otherwise beneficial collaborative activities as a result of competitive pressure', the PMSU paper identifies 'a role for government and the commissioners of public services in ensuring that the right incentives are put in place' to make sure that collaboration is supported (ibid.: 57).

(iii) Users shaping the service from below

'Choice and voice' for users essentially refers to three main processes:

- Providing opportunities for *individual* or *collective user choice* over how public services are delivered. This is closely linked to the idea of *personalisation*, which refers to the tailoring of services to the needs and preferences of individual users. Personalisation has featured particularly strongly in education, where it has meant 'tailoring education to an individual's needs, interests and aptitudes so as to develop better every young person's potential' (ibid.: 64).

- *Funding following users' choices* represents the key mechanism through which bottom-up pressure of user choice combines with the horizontal pressure of competition, forcing public service providers to be responsive to individuals' needs and preferences (or face a loss of funding as service users choose to go elsewhere instead).

- *Engaging users' voice* is concerned with enabling 'users of local public services to express their views about the effectiveness of services, to complain and seek redress if things go wrong and to press for improvements where providers underperform' (ibid.: 64). 'User engagement' also refers to processes of *co-production*, in which citizens actively participate in the production of services, from volunteering and participation in community governance through to 'parental involvement in their child's education, individuals looking after their health, or patients taking more control over their own treatment' (ibid.: 65).

The benefits of harnessing user choice and voice in these ways are claimed to be: greater efficiency, greater collaboration as different providers work together to provide more 'joined-up' services, more responsiveness, improved outcomes, more empowered service users and more equitable outcomes. The potential weaknesses of choice-based systems are identified as being the potential for greater inequity (as the middle classes are often best placed to make choice work to their advantage); increased segregation between social or ethnic groups; or inappropriate outcomes.

As well as steps to ensure equity (such as subsidising transport costs for the less well-off), choice-based systems are also heavily dependent upon full and unbiased information being made available so that users are able to exercise choice and make informed decisions. The most effective way to minimise inequitable outcomes in a choice-based system, of course, is to ensure that all of the choices available are of high quality.

(iv) Capability and capacity

Capability and capacity focus on ensuring that the public service work-force (including the civil service) is equipped to deliver improved public services. Although this aspect of the model is discussed last in the PMSU document, it is argued that

> The quality of service a user experiences depends not only on the level of spending on that service and how its provision is led and organised but on the calibre, skills, attitude, ethos and motivation of the workforce delivering them. For this reason, *front-line and other staff are central to the public services reform agenda.*
>
> (ibid.: 78, emphasis added)

The main elements of capability and capacity within the PMSU document are discussed in more detail at the beginning of Chapter 6.

2.4 Ten assumptions behind the model

We argue that it is possible to discern behind the model a set of implicit assumptions which need to be made explicit. In the following chapters these assumptions are challenged, sometimes because of insufficient evidence, sometimes because the evidence has been misread or used selectively, and sometimes because causal connections have been drawn from weak correlations. In sum, the assumptions represent more an ideological wish list than a set of empirically demonstrated findings:

1. The practices of staff and current methods of teaching are the main factors which need changing and constant pressure and support are required to ensure that they are changed continuously.

2. Slow, incremental change is an inadequate response to the urgent need to raise standards and levels of attainment. Only swift, 'transformational' change will do.

3. Competition, despite its limitations, produces both higher quality results and permanent innovation.

4. The market is the most efficient, effective and equitable means of organising provision.

5. Change can be achieved by giving individuals the power of choice. To enable individuals to exercise choice, a range of providers must exist. If it does not exist, a market needs to be created by encouraging new providers.

6. The private firm offers the most appropriate model for public sector organisations.

7. Although performance indicators produce perverse as well as beneficial outcomes, incentives can be designed to counteract negative effects and to maximise improvements in performance.

8. 'Best practice' can be readily identified and quickly disseminated throughout the education system.

9. The limits of top-down performance management have been recognised, but the centre still retains the right to impose its will upon the system.

10. Policy-makers are able to control institutional leaders and managers, who in turn are able to control teachers.

The four chapters which follow examine in turn the four main features of the new model of reform as they affect different phases within education. Chapter 3 explains the limits of top-down performance management in relation to literacy policy. The limitations of applying market principles in education are then explored in Chapter 4. Whether the current opportunities for parents to exercise voice in their children's schooling are a sufficiently strong mechanism for change is considered in Chapter 5. Finally, Chapter 6 argues, from examples taken from the post-compulsory sector, that staff are being invited to buy into a model of reform that has been decided upon centrally.

3 Understanding the limits of top-down management: literacy policy as a telling case

Gemma Moss

3.1 Introduction

The PMSU paper takes as one of its main themes the limitations of the top-down performance management extensively used by New Labour to manage the public sector since their election in 1997. Open and honest reflection by government on the weaknesses of this approach as well as its strengths is to be welcomed. However, if the document is to set the appropriate agenda for change, then it needs to demonstrate that the right lessons have been learnt from what has gone before. This chapter will use the government's approach to literacy policy – and in particular its flagship programme, the National Literacy Strategy (NLS), now reorganised into the Primary National Strategy (PNS) – as an example of top-down performance management in the public sector. It will ask whether the analysis put forward in the document really reflects the strengths and weaknesses of the policy as it has unfolded, or whether there are omissions in that account that prevent other options from being fully explored.

One of the points raised is whether the government's main motive for moving away from top-down performance management at this stage in the policy cycle stems from the political risks that have now accrued to them as a direct consequence of their centralised approach to public service management. This approach has not always led to services responding as they would have wished. Certainly, the emphasis in the document on the political importance of renewal, and of being seen to still have ideas that can continuously translate into new policies suggest that the priority for politicians really lies with the logic of the political sphere, rather than with the immediate needs of either service providers or service users. The mantra of choice can be read as simply providing government with the justification to do more new things more rapidly, rather than helping to deliver the kind of high-quality service provision that comes from professional commitment and continuity developed over the longer term.

Running day-to-day management of the service according to the priorities of the political sphere carries the risk of substantially distorting public sector practice. One way of testing in whose interests the new model of service reform really works is to review the extent to which present difficulties with the existing round of reform have really been understood. Does the document contain an adequate analysis of the real consequences of the performance culture that the government has already put in place in the public sector, or do the difficulties with this approach remain largely invisible from their vantage point? If the latter is the case, then the document will not be able to suggest an appropriate strategy to correct or address current deficiencies. This chapter will pursue this argument in relation to literacy policy.

3.2 Evidence of success

The Literacy and Numeracy Strategies are invoked as examples of successful and appropriate top-down performance management six times in the document. The evidence quoted to support this point of view are improvements in key performance indicators, such as:

> The number of pupils reaching the expected level in English at age 11 has risen by 14 percentage points to 79% in 2005 and the number reaching the expected level in maths at that age has risen 16 percentage points to 75% in 2005... . Ofsted reports the proportion

of good or excellent teaching in primary schools rising from 45% in 1997 to 74% in 2004/5, and from 59% to 78% in secondary schools. The proportion of badly taught lessons has been halved.

(PMSU 2006a: 36 and 39)

These are substantial achievements. However, the presentation of the evidence masks the fact that most improvement was made in the first few years of the implementation of this top-down process of reform. Since 2000 improvement to pupil performance has been much more modest, and at times resistant to change. The most recent data from the DfES (2006) confirms this (see Figure 3).

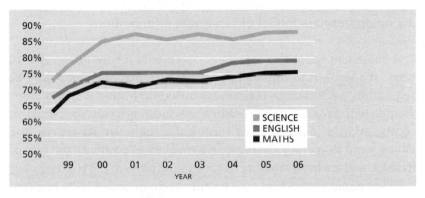

Figure 3 Pupils reaching Level 4 in National Curriculum tests (DfES 2006)

The impact of large-scale reform programmes on measurable outcomes in the education system has been the subject of considerable debate within the academic community, both in the UK and elsewhere. While these issues may not have been fully resolved, the pattern of improvement seen in the NLS is consistent with the achievement of other reform programmes, whatever their starting point or the particular approach adopted (see for example, Linn 2000 for analysis of test data in the USA). The pattern of early gains which subsequently stall can be read as evidence that (a) teachers become more skilled at preparing students for the particular tests introduced with the reform;

or (b) that the reform programme may have successfully eliminated worst practice without significantly enhancing best practice. If the learning environment was significantly enhanced for all pupils, incremental gains sustained over time would generate a different pattern of outcomes (Thompson and Wiliam 2007). Recognising both the initial impact of the Strategies and the difficulties there have been in maintaining that rate of improvement is crucial to understanding both the limits of what such a top-down approach can achieve, and what might most reasonably follow.

3.3 An appropriate model of top-down intervention?

The document identifies four key ingredients in the government's original approach to top-down performance management: targets; regulation; performance assessment including inspection; and intervention with failing providers. While the document concedes that this combination of management tools has largely run its course, the Literacy and Numeracy Strategies are invoked as positive examples of its value and are used to justify its continuing place as part of the policy mix. The paper argues that such an approach continues to be relevant whenever there is a need to clearly prescribe basic service levels, ensure the wider adoption of best practice and ensure uniformity of provision. Yet the actual effect of this kind of performance management on teaching and learning is never fully explored. The only drawback explicitly linked to the Strategies are Ofsted's finding that literacy and numeracy targets may have narrowed the focus of the curriculum at the expense of other subjects. Cited as an example of top-down pressures 'limit[ing] space for innovation and foster[ing] a one-size-fits-all approach which fails to reflect individual or local needs', the report simply adds that this 'is not necessarily the wrong outcome, given the need to raise basic standards' (PMSU 2006a: 40–41). Any further considerations are dismissed.

This is symptomatic of the report as a whole, in so far as it says a good deal about what central government thinks about management, but very little about the effect of that management on the core business of the service involved. The role of management is simply to exert pressure for reform on the workforce. Pressure is deemed to be effective if it improves measurable outcomes. The new model substitutes new forms of horizontal or bottom-up pressure for those previously exerted from the centre, whilst maintaining its own right to intervene. The success of the intervention continues to be judged according to relatively crude numerical measures. Yet the report makes no mention of the fact that the original targets for Literacy (80% reaching Level 4) have still not been met, still less the revised targets of 85% for both Literacy and Numeracy set within the Primary National Strategy. It thus ignores one of the crucial elements that should be taken into account in any thorough assessment of the policy's strengths and weaknesses.

3.4 Recognising the limitations of top-down performance management regimes: what it is possible to see from the centre

Of course, in one sense this kind of selective reference to the Literacy and Numeracy Strategies is entirely justified in a document which seeks to manage a change of gear in the government's approach to public service reform as a whole. The issues are considerably broader than the Strategies themselves, and the focus is on redefining government's management role. From the authors' perspective, it is both important to defend the approach already adopted, while arguing for change.

The new model put forward is certainly built on recognition of some difficulties with the approaches adopted so far, and some ideas about how those difficulties could be solved. Weaknesses recognised in the document include the potential they have to: increase bureaucracy; stifle innovation and foster a one-size-fits-all approach which fails to reflect individual or local needs; create perverse incentives; and disempower professionals. These are attributes which describe the workforce, its relationship to what it does, and, to a much lesser extent, its interaction with service users. Introducing horizontal and bottom-up pressure alongside support for increased capacity is intended to correct the distorting effects of too much centralised control, while making the workforce more responsive to these new stakeholders. This analysis significantly underestimates the difficulties the current insistence on creating a pressure-driven system of reform has in itself created. It also significantly overestimates the extent to which new sources of pressure will do any better at transforming the service than the old. Part of the effect of the model is simply to reduce the overall responsibility for what happens, currently held at the centre, by dispersing it to other sites. This resolves some of the difficulties those at the centre face. It is less likely to help those involved in actual service delivery.

3.5 Applying the PSMU model to the development of the Literacy and Numeracy Strategies

The characteristic features of top-down performance management outlined in the document – targets, regulation, performance assessment including inspection and intervention with failing providers – were an integral part of the Strategies (hereafter referred to as PNS) at their inception. They also included a much larger element of positive support for capacity-building across the system, in line with the revised model. Early evaluations showed that PNS had largely managed to standardise classroom practice and that this happened during the first period of implementation when results rose fastest (DfES 2003; OISE 2003; Ofsted 2002a). Yet it is also possible to argue that such a high degree of standardisation was only achieved at the expense of many of the features described in the report as inherent weaknesses in top-down management systems: increased bureaucracy; a one-size-fits-all approach which fails to reflect individual or local needs; leading to perverse incentives and disempowered professionals. Indeed by 2003 the publication of *Excellence and Enjoyment* (DfES 2003) clearly signalled that those involved at the centre within the DfES and the PNS both recognised and were trying to tackle precisely this range of issues. In many respects *Excellence and Enjoyment* therefore anticipates some of the analysis of the failings of top-down performance management made in the PMSU discussion paper, and already looks for other ways of managing service improvement. This makes PNS a particularly interesting point of comparison.

3.6 Command and control as the spur for innovation

One of the core weaknesses government now sees in the process of top-down performance management is that it stifles innovation. But a review of PNS and its evolution shows that as a top-down system it did not stifle innovation per se. On the contrary, while the initial standardisation of classroom delivery may have explicitly constrained innovation at the level of service deliverers, it positively encouraged innovation at the level of the central management team. As results continued to plateau, the team became extremely adept at identifying further avenues to explore which might lead to better performance outcomes. The development of the Strategies is in fact one of continual innovation in precisely this area.

What the history of PNS also shows is that innovation, when driven at the speed at which managers at the centre can process performance data and then try to adjust the system in the timeframe of the annual review, actually creates further dilemmas for those working in such a heavily regulated and target-driven regime. Each successive wave of reform has less and less chance of really bedding down, as basic goals and aims are re-shaped. Faced with the continued pressure of meeting higher targets, many schools either experiment wildly, grasping at any innovation which might seem to promise quick results – brain gym, water bottles, the latest phonics scheme – or, unable to choose between the baffling array of ideas and the speed at which they change, schools stick to the most heavily standardised and conservative line of practice that they can find, most obviously the most clearly delineated model of practice disseminated at the beginning of the Strategy.

One of the most perverse consequences of this kind of top-down pressure is that it has indeed stifled meaningful innovation by innovating too fast at the centre on too short timelines, with too little regard for what is really needed or possible in specific local circumstances. Overvalorising innovation itself causes difficulties. (It is noticeable that Ofsted's review of *The Curriculum in Successful Primary Schools* (Ofsted 2002b) concludes that one of the features of such institutions is that they are highly selective about the initiatives they commit time and effort to.) Yet the difficulties in gearing the pace of policy change at the centre with the pace of meaningful reform within the institutions charged with carrying such policies out is hard for those at the centre to see.

There is a kind of inherent logic to 'doing more' built into the structures which currently drive reform. Departments of State are increasingly driven by ministers' needs to show that the pace of change has not slowed down under their watch, compounded by Number Ten's demands for new initiatives to feed the media. The financial control exerted over policy from the Treasury does not mitigate this state of affairs. Within the field of education, the Treasury funds initiatives. It does so by setting aside funding streams to pursue particular kinds of policy objectives, whose success can then be scrutinised through transparent evaluation. Unfortunately this is often expected to take place within relatively short timeframes. A perfectly laudable aim in itself, it has actually led to policy proliferation as the many different agencies already charged with a particular aspect of policy each vie to have their own ideas adopted. Ministers' needs to find new policy initiatives are precisely fed in this way. Choosing what to do next has indeed become a core part of government activity.

Growth in government-funded activity of this kind can be demonstrated by: the rise in the number of agencies charged with carrying out different aspects of education policy; the rise in the number of policy documents such agencies produce (Ofsted published 11 documents in 1997, 10 in 1998, and 326 by 2004); and the volume of policy documentation tied into specific funding streams now disseminated into schools (see the Standards website). A core part of public sector activity is simply trying to keep up with what the service is being asked and expected to do by outside agencies who may in themselves have very limited understanding of local circumstances or priorities, let alone the core relationship between service providers and users at that level.

3.7 Would the PMSU prescription for a new model of reform help solve the dilemmas that the PNS ran into?

The answer to this question really depends on what one thinks those dilemmas are. From the point of view of government the greatest political difficulty with PNS is that it has never fully met the original targets. This leaves the government vulnerable to the suggestion that a large number of children leave primary school without basic literacy or numeracy skills (see for instance the Public Accounts Committee discussion of literacy attainment in Northern Ireland).[1] Such an assertion is based on a complete misunderstanding of what Level 4 at Key Stage 2 means. But this cannot be unpicked, given the way in which the government have so clearly identified Level 4 attainment at KS2 as the necessary prerequisite for making adequate progress at KS3. The government target and the pressure on the system it was designed to enforce have distorted debate on the issues. This in turn has completely clouded thinking about where to go next. The sequence of events leading up to the instigation of the Rose Review and the incorporation of its findings into the revised curriculum framework for literacy lays bare many of the difficulties here.

3.8 The turn to phonics in the context of the policy cycle

The Rose Review and the outcomes it has led to are mentioned in the document as an example of the continuing need for government to sometimes 'simply take a top-down approach and require the adoption of best practice' (PMSU 2006a: 58). Such action is counterpoised to the potential uneven diffusion of best practice at a horizontal level without this kind of direct intervention. Box 6.14 in the PMSU document represents the Rose Review as the outcome of a research-led process in which: 'to ensure that children in England have the best opportunity to read, this year the Government has made a commitment to make synthetic phonics the prime method of teaching reading across the country' (ibid.).

In fact the Rose Review derived, not from systematic research undertaken on phonics (see Torgerson *et al.* 2006) nor any research assessment of its relevance to the relative success of the NLS, but from the political process at Westminster. In a context where the Literacy Strategy had still failed to meet its targets, a small-scale intervention in Clackmannanshire (Johnston and Watson 2005), which would not have met the criteria for inclusion in a systematic literature review, became the means for political opponents to berate the poor progress and poor returns from Labour's education policy. Running in parallel to a number of other interventions aimed at boosting pupil performance in the same schools, the significance of such a small-scale study's findings would not have had the same weight at an earlier point in the policy cycle.

As it was, the opposition nominated the issue of how best to teach reading as the subject of enquiry for the Education and Skills Committee in the House of Commons and used the Clackmannanshire findings to attack the government's record on the literacy curriculum. This set in motion the sequence of events which led to the political decision to institute the Rose Review and all the outcomes that have followed. While not wishing in any way to impugn the quality of the evidence presented to the Committee, the process through which the Committee itself deliberated, or the subsequent conduct of the Rose Review, we argue that this is a very different means of arriving at a definition of 'best practice' in a substantive area of professional practice than the procedures used in the Health Service via the National Institute of Health and Clinical Excellence (NICE). In the latter case these include safeguards against undue influence being exerted by lobbying, media coverage or special-interest groups in the recognition that these risk distorting professional practice.

It is a moot point whether the 'commitment to make synthetic phonics the prime method of teaching reading across the country' really equates to the adoption of best practice, rather than the imposition of a 'one-size-fits-all approach which fails to reflect individual or local needs' (PMSU 2006a: 58 and 40). There is to date no evidence that this really is the crucial missing ingredient that will address the plateau in results. In fact, results for KS2 in 2005 show that 84% of children already reach Level 4 in reading, with 90% already reaching Level 3 and above. The real difficulty in raising literacy attainment rests with the writing curriculum, where outcomes continue to lag behind. If Ofsted had for some time raised the issue of the quality of phonics teaching in the NLS, then its concerns were less to do with the methods espoused within the NLS and the materials it provided than with the way in which schools acted on that advice, a point made clear in the evidence given to the Education and Skills Committee by the then Chief Inspector, David Bell.

3.9 Tackling education reform north and south of the border

It is notable that in Scotland itself the Clackmannanshire study has had hardly any impact on practice. Weighed against other initiatives taking place at the same time it was seen to have led to some modest gains in a quite specific area of literacy skills which were largely washed out by the end of primary education. But Scotland also has in place a very different set of relationships between politicians and those charged with improving schools. In particular, while schools themselves do closely monitor pupil progress and can be held to account for pupil performance by both Local Authorities (LAs) and the school inspectorate (HMIE), politicians monitor education system performance via the Programme for International Student Assessment (PISA) and the Progress in International Reading Literacy Study (PIRLS), large-scale comparative studies of a statistically reliable sample of Scottish pupils, conducted every few years. Consequently, politicians are not directly accountable for meeting pupil performance targets in the way that their counterparts south of the border are, and do not feel the same kind of need to champion one pedagogy over another, or face the political risks of having made the 'wrong' choice. Pedagogy in Scotland remains much more clearly a matter of professional judgement.

Where politicians do get involved is by earmarking funds for school improvement in areas that they identify as a priority for the system as a whole, e.g. monies were set aside for work on Early Years, the funding stream which among many others supported the Clackmannanshire study. LAs, schools and partners in HEI bid for the funds to carry out initiatives designed to generate new knowledge and improve practice in these areas. These are then evaluated. That means that policies for school improvement happen at a scale that schools and LAs have the ability and willingness to invest in. The kinds of difficulties in gearing activity at the centre with activity in local settings, experienced in the English system, are not in evidence here. Of course other difficulties remain. In particular the question of how to spread best practice. Whilst there is acceptance that what may work well in one setting may not necessarily travel elsewhere, the question of how to level up performance across the system as a whole remains a key issue.

As a key driver for tackling underperformance in the Scottish system, considerable effort has gone into ensuring that the various agencies working on education coordinate their input and responsibilities. In large part this has been achieved by establishing a robust consensus over the form of school evaluation that acts as the driver for school improvement, while clearly delineating the various roles and responsibilities of all those involved. This has been done by using a single policy document: *How good is our school?* (HMIE 2002) as the means of coordinating the input of all the key stakeholders in the process of school improvement. This document encourages schools to use a variety of indicators to examine their performance in all key areas of their work. Pupil performance is one of the indicators used, but takes its place alongside others. This mitigates any distorting effects on school practice of using numerical outputs as the sole measure of teaching and learning quality. Coordinated use of this approach to system reform means that the pace of innovation matches rather than outstrips the local capacity to make lasting change.

3.10 When to intervene, when not to intervene: balancing pressures on service delivery

The performance data collected since the introduction of both Literacy and Numeracy Strategies suggest that they had most influence on outcomes in the early stages when they did most to standardise practice amongst different service providers. The data suggest that this kind of top-down performance management has an impact over a finite time period. Once the initial process of standardisation was complete, the Strategies have shown a much more modest influence on outcomes. This is despite a continual flow of innovations and adjustments. Pressure in the system, whether top-down, horizontal or bottom-up, has created a context where continual innovation is both sought after and treated as a good. The PMSU document talks of creating a 'self-improving' system with incentives for continuous improvement and innovation. Valorising innovation above other virtues such as consistency or quality ensures a semblance of continual activity which may indeed be an asset in political circles. It is less clear that it helps maintain a high-quality education system that runs in the interests of its users.

While the model of service reform offered in the PMSU document in one sense abrogates power from the centre, it in fact largely panders to those who exercise most political control over events and leaves room for the centre to take power back to itself, as and when the political climate demands it. It is not able to deal with the bigger questions, in particular how to create new forms of curriculum knowledge and an enhanced quality of teaching and learning which may really meet the needs of new kinds of economic relations within the wider society.

3.11 Implications for policy

- Top-down performance management may have a role in standardising basic aspects of service delivery, but such a role is time-limited. Those adopting such an approach need to build in a timetable which includes clear handover and exit strategies from over-reliance on this form of management.

- Pressure-driven systems bring with them a number of risks which cannot be mitigated by changing the direction in which pressure is applied. Pressure-driven reform is possible when there are clear solutions to well-specified problems in service quality that are ready and waiting to be shared. But continual pressure does not help build the kind of professional knowledge required to address more intractable and deep-seated difficulties. Arguably, this point has been reached in education, where the real difficulties lie in imagining the kind of curriculum which is fit for purpose in a rapidly changing society.

- There are real and substantial distorting effects that stem from conflating action in the political sphere with action in the sphere of professional practice. While politicians can set a general direction in which a substantial area of professional practice should evolve, they cannot micro-manage the means by which the service will get there, nor specify the precise route to be taken.

- Innovation should not automatically be valued over and above consistency and quality in any process of reform. Successive policy innovation on short timescales militates against deep rather than superficial service improvements. Responsibility for determining the balance between change and continuity needs to be shared more equally between professionals and other stakeholders.

- Models of professional accountability which lead to system improvement do not have to be externally driven, nor give most power to those who know least about professional practice. Scotland provides an interesting alternative to the English system of accountability, and should be more fully explored by policy-makers south of the border.

Note
1 See http://www.publications.parliament.uk/pa/cm200607/cmselect/cmpubacc/108/6062101.htm

4 Market incentives in schools

Rebecca Allen and Anna Vignoles

4.1 Introduction

The PMSU discussion paper makes the case that marketisation of the education system will improve standards in education, whilst maintaining or even improving equity of access. While we have sympathy with the notion that we want to empower children, or rather their parents, in order to improve the accountability of schools and the educational experiences of their pupils, at a theoretical level there are a number of potential limitations to the application of market principles in education.

Marketisation and choice are appealing to policy-makers perhaps because it feels like a potential one-stop solution to the ongoing challenge of raising educational standards. Marketisation will, it is argued, empower parents and give schools greater autonomy to respond to parents. It will therefore alleviate the need for state action at a local level, which may not suit all school contexts and can often cause unpredictable knock-on problems in the system. However, for marketisation to work, even at a theoretical level, schools must have a clear incentive to expand – and they must also be able to contract and shut down. Yet expansion in the UK post-1988 has been moderate, and school closure has been heavily controlled. Only 120 schools applied to increase their capacity in the UK between 1999 and 2005 (Select Committee for Education and Skills 2005).

Secondly, parents need to choose schools on the basis of accurate information about school quality. Yet even with abundant information on schools available to parents, it is not clear whether parents choose on the basis of effectiveness (as measured by value added) or peer group (overall league table position) or proximity, or some mixture of these and other criteria. If parents choose on the basis of overall league table rankings, this provides an incentive for schools to 'cream skim' more-able children, with potential for increased ability and socio-economic segregation across schools.

Thirdly, it is assumed that teachers and head teachers will respond to market pressures by increasing their efforts and raising standards. Yet it is not even clear what the objectives of decision-makers in schools actually are (Dixit 2002; Besley and Ghatak 2003). Certainly there are multiple outputs from the education system, and so it is not clear what teachers, head teachers and parents would like to maximise.

4.2 PMSU summary of the evidence base

The evidence on the benefits of school competition that are cited in the PMSU discussion paper comes largely from the US (Hoxby 2003a; Greene and Winters 2004) and from Sweden (Sandstrom and Bergstrom 2005; Ahlin 2003; Bjorklund *et al.* 2004). However, the examples cited are selective and are a misleading reading of the literature as a whole. A small positive association between competition and pupil outcomes has indeed been found in many US studies (Belfield and Levin 2003), but few of these studies infer that this is a causal effect. Studies that do claim a causal relationship are hotly contested in the literature (Hoxby 2000, 2005; Rothstein 2005). There is an emerging literature that looks at the effect of Charter schools[1] on the performance of all pupils living in an area. Of the three major studies published so far, one finds a posi-tive effect of Charter school competition on other public schools (Booker *et al.* 2005) and two find no effect (Buddin and Zimmer 2005; Bettinger 2005). Likewise the evidence from Sweden is not as positive as the PMSU states. Of the three studies they quote, only one finds a consistently positive relationship between competition from private schools and pupil performance (Sandstrom and Bergstrom, 2005). This study is somewhat weaker in terms of data quality and methods, however (Allen 2007b). From the other two studies we can conclude that the effect of private school competition on public schools is either zero, or very small indeed in maths with no effect in other subjects.

In any case, the potential competition effects from marketisation of school systems are likely to be quite specific to the institutional setting. Evidence from the US[2] is of limited applicability in the UK due to the very different nature of the schooling system. Most competition studies from the US are taken from an institution setting whereby parents must move into the neighbourhood to access their desired school; this is very different to the English conception of parental choice. Furthermore, the funding allocation mechanisms across the two countries are very different. Funding for US schools is largely locally raised, while funding for schools in the UK primarily comes from national taxation. This means that in the US, funding per student in wealthier areas is considerably higher than in poorer areas. By contrast, in the UK, funding is generally given more generously to areas with higher levels of deprivation. Other differences in school governance and control, as well as operation of catchment areas, mean that evaluations of school choice or voucher schemes from the US may not necessarily tell us much about the impact of school choice in a UK context.

There is in fact a much more relevant and more extensive UK evidence base on the impact of marketisation on both equity and efficiency that the PMSU draws on only partially, as we shall show below.

4.3 School choice in the UK

Whether or not parents genuinely want school choice, as opposed to simply wanting their nearest school to be of high quality, is an unresolved question. Certainly the extent of school choice in the UK is a contentious issue. Recent work by Burgess *et al.* (2007) suggests that school choice was being exercised by around half of children in the UK (or their parents). However, Allen (2007a) suggests that, at most, only one in five children are benefiting from the 'right to choose' reforms which were implemented after 1988. Choice is a possibility for some parents – but by no means all.

Different types of parents are differently informed about schools and may have different preferences and thus make different choices (Hastings *et al.* 2005; West and Pennell 1999). There is evidence that the nature and motivations behind particular school choice decisions differ for parents from more or less socio-economically advantaged backgrounds (see for example Coldon and Boulton 1991; West and Varlaam 1991). This evidence tentatively suggests that higher socio-economic group parents have access to more information on the nature of the choices available to them and the quality of schools that they can access. Such parents may therefore be more effective in getting their children into higher performing schools. More successful schools will hence tend disproportionately to attract advantaged children who will, on average, be higher achievers. This will worsen any tendency for a child's socio-economic background and the education and attitudes of their parents to determine their attainment, as opposed to the ability or effort of the child (Brown 1998: 393). Of course it has to be said that even without a school choice system, children who have wealthy parents, who can move into the catchment area of a good school and who invest more in their children's schooling, will tend to achieve more. School choice may exacerbate this however.

4.4 Marketisation and equity

Even in the absence of 'school choice', schools in the UK were socio-economically segregated pre-1988. Parents moved house to access better schools and there is clear evidence that parents are prepared to pay for higher school standards, in the form of larger mortgages (see Black 1999 for the US, and Gibbons and Machin 2006 for the UK).

The PMSU discussion paper claims that 'under certain circumstances choice can lead to more equitable outcomes' (PMSU 2006a: 68), citing Arend and Lent (2004) and Hoxby (2003b). Socio-economic segregation across schools did fall between 1991 and 1993, but, contrary to what is claimed by the PMSU, this was almost certainly not the result of the choice reforms (Allen and Vignoles 2007) but rather due to measurement issues. In any case, despite methodological disagreements, all researchers agree that school segregation has been slowly rising since 1994 (Gorard *et al.* 2002; Allen and Vignoles forthcoming; Goldstein and Noden 2003; Noden 2000). Furthermore, school segregation has risen faster in London, where school choice is most developed, than in other regions (Allen and Vignoles 2007). One explanation for the fact that school segregation did not initially increase post-1988 is that school choice was already happening prior to 1988, via parents' choice of house location. The introduction of choice would have had minimal impact on segregation if the most popular schools were unable to expand capacity – which, as discussed earlier, seems likely. A second possibility is that choice has genuinely increased but that this has not led to increased segregation. This implies that poorer parents are able to make similar school choices to richer parents. We do not have the evidence to distinguish between these two explanations. However, if the former explanation is correct, as school rolls fall over the next few years and spaces become available in schools, then we would expect to see rising segregation as more able or wealthier children take these spare places in the most popular schools.

There is evidence that existing admission practices under the UK choice regime may increase social segregation across schools. West *et al.*'s analysis (2004) of comprehensive secondary school admissions criteria in England reveals a significant minority of (mostly voluntary-aided and foundation) schools using criteria, such as demonstrable religiosity, that appear to be designed potentially to select a certain group of pupils and so exclude others. Allen (2007a) shows that a large proportion of these admissions-controlling schools are successful in achieving a pupil intake of higher ability and social status than if they had accepted the pupils who live nearest to their school. Not all of these practices will be restricted under the new proposed Code of Practice. For instance, schools can still require parents to prove the extent of their religiosity.

4.5 Marketisation and pupil performance

The UK evidence on the effects of competition does not suggest that marketisation has brought substantial improvements in pupil perform-ance. There are only two reasonably positive results (from Bradley *et al.* 2001 and Levačić 2004), and these are now quite old, using data that is inferior to the post-2001 pupil-level data. The PMSU discussion paper claims that Gibbons *et al.* (2005) support the view that competition improves pupil outcomes: this is a misreading of this paper. Their main result is of no overall effect of choice or competition on performance. Some very small positive effect of competition only relates to religious schools. Recent quasi-experimental papers fail to find an effect of competition on pupil performance in England (Burgess and Slater 2006; Clark 2004).

So why might competition not lead to higher achievement in schools? First, as discussed, if parental choice is very limited then we would not expect to see extensive competition, at least not across all schools. Furthermore, for choice and competition to lead to higher achievement in schools, the incentives for head teachers and teachers need to be aligned such that all involved respond to competition by making efforts to 'raise standards', however that may be defined. The extent to which the current system of tempered competition – between some but, of course, not all schools – provides clear incentives for teachers to improve standards is not obvious. For instance, head teachers in certain rural areas may face little competition for their students, almost regardless of the performance of their school.

4.6 Implications for policy

- The PMSU has cited selectively from the evidence base to propose policies to encourage still greater levels of marketisation in the school system. They make the argument that choice of school causes schools to compete and hence become more efficient, raising standards of pupil attainment. This optimistic view is not supported by our reading of the evidence base.

- The causal impact of choice and competition on attainment remains unproven, at least in the context of the current system in the UK.

- School choice, to date at least, has not led to substantial increases in segregation across schools. This does not imply that the current system is equitable, in terms of access to good quality schools, but rather that school choice has not worsened the level of socio-economic segregation across schools.

- School choice in its current form is quite limited in the UK. Good schools are full and parents can only access such schools by living extremely close by. This proximity system of allocating school places has always operated in the UK and, if school choice reform has not altered this system, we would not anticipate big changes in the level of segregation.

- Over the next decade or so, pupil numbers will fall. This will allow greater parental choice and, by implication, increase the scope for both equity losses and efficiency gains. There will be a clearer equity–efficiency trade-off and we are likely to observe either gains in standards due to genuine competition, or increasing social stratification across schools, or both.

- As the potential for competition increases, so greater efforts must be made to limit selection by schools (as opposed to selection by parents).

- The current government's commitment not to allow increased 'ability selection' by schools, combined with changes to the admissions code, is an attempt to guard against selection by schools. It remains to be seen, however, whether subsequent governments start to allow schools more unfettered control over their own admissions, again with the likely consequence of greater social stratification.

- Even in the absence of formal 'ability selection' or parental interviews, schools that control their own admissions do appear to have the means to be more selective than their formal criteria would suggest. Other mechanisms to determine admission in the case of oversubscription need therefore to be considered, such as lotteries.

- The role of faith schools in the system also needs to be debated. Specifically, one might consider only allowing faith schools to use a binary indicator of whether someone is of that particular faith or not. Currently, faith schools are allowed to treat religiosity as a continuous measure and they are therefore allowed to select from within the faith group children whose parents show a greater degree of overt and documented religiosity. This may disadvantage lower socio-economic background children who are of that particular faith but whose religiosity is not so readily documented.

Notes
1 Charter schools are non-sectarian public schools operated privately. Such schools are accountable to the state or local school board and usually have a contract stating the school's mission, students served, methods of assessment used, etc.
2 There is a large body of international evidence on choice from the US, New Zealand, Australia, Sweden, Denmark, Colombia and Chile. Many US studies are restricted to looking at effects on pupils who experience choice, e.g. Rouse (1998) for Milwaukee voucher program; Krueger and Zhu (2004) for New York voucher program; Cullen *et al.* (2005) for Charter schools. Other US studies focus on the impact of choice on the whole system, e.g. Hoxby (2003b); Bayer and McMillan (2005); Bettinger (2005); Booker *et al.* (2005).

5 Parental voice in education

Carol Vincent

5.1 Introduction

Voice is discussed, along with choice, in Chapter 7 of the document, *The UK Government's Approach to Public Service Reform* (PMSU 2006a). Both are presented as 'bottom-up pressures' allowing 'users to shape the service from below'. Rather more space and consideration is given to choice than voice, and this reflects the degree to which choice is already embedded in government policy and practice with regard to public services. Voice is described as complementary to choice – and as 'a way of registering discontent and securing change to avoid failure' (ibid.: 65). This throws some light onto the version of voice presented here; namely a consumerist conception that allows individuals to become 'more assertive customers' (ibid.: 65). This understanding is different to the one that we will suggest here, which focuses on user participation in shaping educational and other public sector services. This second reading of voice is briefly recognised in the document, as the next step on from consumer comment. 'Assertive customers can become active participants or citizens by taking greater responsibility for delivering services or increasing the chances of services producing positive outcomes. This is called co-production' (ibid.: 65). Co-production, or elsewhere what is referred to as 'loud' voice (ibid.: 64), will be discussed below, but the nub of our argument here is that the idea of user participation is not explored in any depth or detail by PMSU, and thus remains, in the confines of this document, a rather empty concept.

5.2 Current opportunities to exercise voice in education

It is important to first note that in relation to education the 'users' whose involvement is discussed are often parents, rather than children. The exercise of student voice raises a rather different set of issues, as does that of teacher voice (Hargreaves 1996) and for reasons of space, this chapter will concentrate on parental voice, involvement and participation.

Voice and choice are linked in the PMSU document, but we suggest, here and in Chapter 4, that they are two very different concepts. 'Voice' is a more unfamiliar response than 'exit' for many clients, more 'messy', and more uncertain in its outcome (Hirschman 1970). Hirschman famously described voice as follows:

> To resort to voice, rather than exit is for the customer or member to make an attempt at changing the practices, policies and outputs of the firm from which one buys or the organisation to which one belongs. Voice here is defined as any attempt at all to change, rather than escape from, an objectionable state of affairs, whether through individual or collective petition.
>
> (1970: 30)

We argue that the opportunities for the exercise of individual or collective parental voice *within* a school are currently limited, and that there is an absence of concrete proposals in the PMSU paper to ameliorate this situation. Buckley's (2007) recent research in the US points to the way in which schools, teachers and other education professionals and institutions seek to limit the range of issues on which the exercise of parental voice is seen as appropriate. Summarising a position remarkably similar to that proffered by the PMSU discussion paper, Buckley states, 'This vision of effective schools means that stakeholders work together to co-produce higher quality education, making the relationship between parents, students and teachers more co-operative and inter-dependent' (2007: 4). This casual relationship is thought to exist because the chosen schools wish to keep their consumers or (more accurately) their parents satisfied, and therefore staff are more closely accountable to parents (see also PMSU ch. 7). Buckley's research focuses on examining the assumption that school choice will transform parents from passive clients of a government service to 'active partners, entitled to a say in how schools are run and how students are taught' (2007: 5). He questions the assumed relationship between choice and voice, and also points to the way in which parental propensity to exercise voice is socially structured. It is worth noting that his identification of two main types of involvement – attendance at meetings and volunteering – may in themselves offer only limited opportunities for the exercise of voice. The former has perhaps the potential for participation, the latter very little. His results suggest a mixed picture with increases and decreases in these two main types of involvement, across different types of choice school.[1] These variations serve to question the easy linkages assumed by PMSU between choice and voice. Buckley goes on to suggest that schools demonstrate a

> lack of receptivity to parental efforts to influence school operations –
> that is, the schools may be making it clear that input and
> participation above a certain level is unwanted. As Hirschman (1970)
> observes in his classic book, *Exit, Voice, and Loyalty*, institutions
> designed to perfect the 'exit' option, such as educational choice, may
> become increasingly incompatible with the use of 'voice'.
>
> (2007: 12)

Thus while the government may allocate a role for parents as consumers exercising choice, even the successful chooser is not necessarily granted a voice within the chosen school. This is because consumerism rests on the power of 'exit', an economic mechanism that has no necessary nor inevitable relationship with 'voice', a political mechanism. The two can be in tension, as numerous parental exits from a school can lead to weakened capacity for voice (Adler and Raab 1988). Thus a model of contractual relations borrowed from the private sector which locates parents purely as consumers does not fit when applied to public sector schools which demand a more multifaceted response from parents. This argument is consistent with other research conducted in the UK and the US which argues that schools are keen to confine parents to a role as 'supporter/learners' within school (that is, as fundraiser, audience member, volunteer and one who adopts school-approved practices at home) (e.g. Lareau 1989; Woods *et al.* 1998; Vincent 2000; Vincent and Martin 2002; Luttrell 1997; Reay 1998; Crozier 2000; Griffith and Smith 2005; Gillies 2007).

Individual voice

Instances of parental lobbying on behalf of their own child are known to every school, but whether parents possess an effective individual voice (that is, in the sense of a dialogue leading to school activity and change) is largely determined by two sets of factors – the first being the differential possession and activation of individual parents' social, cultural and material resources, and the second, schools' views of what aspects of their children's education parents should be concerned with (Lareau 1989; Vincent and Martin 2002; Vincent 2001).

'Co-production' is defined by PMSU simply as 'parental involvement in their child's education' (2006a: 65), but as we have noted, that involvement is often limited and constrained. The limitations may arise from parental uncertainty or alienation, or professional concern about lay incursion into what appears to be teachers' territory.

We argue that there are a number of elements in play which can be read off from the current policy ensemble as defining 'good' and 'appropriate' parenting roles in relation to school, and that none of them offer more than limited opportunities to exercise individual parental voice. Current policies position parents in three main roles: first as a *consumer* choosing a good education for their child, second, once the child is in school, acting as a *'partner'* with education professionals, largely on the school's terms (witness Home–School Agreements introduced in 1998), and third, the *responsible* parent (see the Home Office's Respect agenda in which the importance of parenting work to develop a reasoning and reasonable child is emphasised)

(Walkerdine and Lucey 1989). The Respect agenda also validates the 'parent as partner' model, designing a 'model partner', with the parent offering help to the school when requested and in support of the education of their own child, rather than wider issues). Parent Councils and Parent Teacher Associations (PTAs), potentially collective forums for parent discussion, are identified in the PMSU diagram of the overall reform model (see Figure 2 in Chapter 2 above), but are not discussed in the text.

Collective voice

The exercise of collective voice is an even more unfamiliar concept for many parents. The clearest example of parents having this opportunity is as parent governors. There is, to date, some evidence to suggest that some parents at least (largely white and middle-class) are taking up the recently accorded rights to participate in school life in the role of active citizen (e.g. Ranson *et al.* 2003). However, these parents remain in a minority, and may find themselves playing marginalised roles on governing bodies (Martin 1999). Parent governors are in any case instructed to see themselves as integral parts of the governing body (Hatcher *et al.* 1993; Deem *et al.* 1995), rather than as representatives of particular interest groups – representative parents, rather than parent representatives. As a result, their links with the parent body of the school are usually weak.

For many parents, the only visible collective space is that offered by the PTA or Friends of the school. These groups are normally concerned with fundraising and arranging social events, and not generally used as discussion forums. The latter is, in fact, relatively uncommon in schools. Attempts have been made to build a different culture, one more supportive of lay participation, in many local programmes run by Sure Start. Guidance was made available to local programmes, as part of the National Evaluation of Sure Start, in order to help professionals make opportunities for the participation of local families 'in the designing, reshaping and the ongoing development of local programmes' (Brodie 2003: 4). Similarly, case studies show local successes in creating a culture where parents are the motivating force behind the creation of particular services, designed to meet perceived local need (e.g. support groups for fathers, Brodie 2003; fruit and vegetable deliveries, community sports events, Williams and Churchill 2006). Such action and involvement can result in personal development for the individual as his/her sense of self-esteem and efficacy grows, as well as small instances of community development, and may (although this is not discussed by Williams and Churchill), lead to professionals adopting more inclusive and dialogic ways of delivering services, having had experience of active parental voice and participation.

5.3 Exercising user voice in education: the complexities and difficulties

Any serious attempt to increase the exercise of parental voice within the education system has to engage with a number of serious complexities and difficulties. Space does not allow an elaboration of these here (see Vincent 1992; Vincent 2000; Vincent and Martin 2002), but they include:

- Professional defensiveness: Resistance may come from professionals who perceive the introduction of lay voices into decision-making in school as a further encroachment on teacher autonomy.

- Lay reluctance: It is an unfamiliar experience for many adults to be asked to participate in public sector services, and some will feel that is not their role to do so (Benhabib 1996).

- Distribution of social and economic resources: Parents have unequal resources with which to exercise voice. Gender, class and ethnicity interact in complex ways to shape modes of participation for individuals.

- Romanticising the exercise of voice: There can be a tendency to overlook illiberal or awkward voices which 'we' do not wish to hear (Hargreaves 1996).

- Diversity of voices: How does one make policy from a plurality of often competing voices?

- The sheer hard work and emotional energy demanded from participants by their involvement in deliberative dialogue.

Although there is a welcome recognition by PMSU that the skills to exercise voice are unevenly distributed across society, and that participation requires the building of individual skills and confidence – a process that needs support – there is no recognition of the complexities inherent in the task, nor suggestions as to how support can be offered: what sort of support, offered by whom, in which forums? Professional support is not unproblematic in itself because there is a risk of achieving only 'unequal networks dominated by professional discourses and practices' (Garmarnikow and Green 2007: 18).

The ability to exercise voice, to participate in initiatives, to engage in dialogue, cannot be abstracted from social and economic inequalities (Garmarnikow and Green 2007). Phillips refers to 'the profound lack of social recognition' (1999: 80) which some individuals and groups experience. She emphasises the economic factors underpinning problems of recognition, and argues that people's sense of political competence, efficacy and even of interest in issues decided outside of the home cannot be divorced from the economic conditions governing their own lives. We agree entirely with Phillips's point here, but in order to engender some debate, we focus, in the next section, on the importance of establishing, encouraging and strengthening locally based deliberative forums. We do so in the belief that the existence and workings of such groups may slowly result in small, but significant changes in expectations, assumptions and procedures around decision-making in state education.

5.4 The potential of school-based parents' groups

At first sight, the potential of school-based parents' groups to make an impact on institutional decision-making does not look promising. Vincent, Ranson and Martin (Vincent and Martin 2002, 2005; Ranson *et al*. 2004) conducted research on school-based parent groups which had a brief to include deliberation and dialogue with staff, in addition to the traditional fundraising role. They argued that attempts to bring parental voices in to decision-making procedures within schools are fragile and highly localised, dependent on the goodwill of 'gate-keepers' such as head teachers, and beset by difficulties such as the challenge of building up a group and retaining a healthy membership. There were instances of professional co-option, whereby parents were not free to determine their own agendas, or where discussion was heavily managed (also, e.g., Fine 1997; Crozier 2000; Armstrong 2003). As noted above, the exercise of voice is also highly mediated by parental possession of social, cultural and economic resources and their willing-ness to activate those resources in their relationship with the school (Lareau 1989; Vincent 2001). However, despite these reservations, the researchers conclude that the parent groups made some progress in creating arenas where lay voices could be injected into what has been hitherto a largely professional preserve.

Given this, we do not overlook the difficulties of putting voice into practice in a meaningful way that also has visible outcomes for partic-ipants; and we acknowledge that these difficulties will always make success in this area partial and fragile. Nonetheless, we argue that discussion and deliberation forums located in schools – despite the many difficulties – offer opportunities for parents to exercise voice. They can give parents the opportunity to act as citizens participating in deliberation and dialogue over issues which concern their children and the school as a whole. Thus such discussions can possess an imme-diacy and degree of familiarity and informality which larger, more impersonal forums, such as Citizens' Juries (PMSU 2006a: 64) or local authority consultations often lack. Meetings arranged in order to shape policy on welfare issues (uniform, behaviour, food at school, and so on) rather than curricular issues can be less threatening for both teachers and parents. Small group discussions as a part of a larger meeting can make it easier for individuals to voice their opinion. A culture needs to be generated that understands that the best that can be hoped for in terms of a 'solution' is a temporary consensus, a temporary settlement around particular issues (Mouffe 1993). These issues may seem trivial, the proposal too mundane, but we believe that it is in small and local forums, discussing matters of everyday relevance to parents, their children and teachers that people learn the exacting and exhausting business of exercising voice and resolving apparent oppositions into workable policies. Making such school-level forums mandatory, and linking their deliberations with those of pupil councils would begin to bring together the range of stakeholders involved in education. A network of parent forums would also allow local authorities to communicate directly with teachers and families in their areas. Such reforms will of course, remain weak if not connected to changes throughout the education system, designed to strengthen democratic accountability.

The formation and spread of such networks and groups also has the potential to develop social capital – that is, strong local networks, a sense of community cohesion, and high degrees of trust and interaction between individuals. The generation of social capital, especially in disadvantaged areas, is understood by New Labour to be key to their policies on reducing social exclusion (Garmarnikow and Green 1999).

Despite the problems outlined above, the operation of such forums may go some way towards the realisation of democratic local learning systems. As Hargreaves suggests, we should 'risk cacophony in our struggle to build … community' (1996: 16). Thus we see great potential in the concept of voice as a lever for reform. However, a simplistic championing of the notion, without a full engagement with the complexities inherent in the concept will, we believe, result only in rhetoric, tokenism and superficiality.

5.5 Implications for policy

- Choice and voice are not – in the version offered by PMSU – strong mechanisms for change in the education system.

- Therefore in order to increase opportunities for exercising voice, radical reform of lay–professional relationships in education is required.

- Requiring the establishment of parent forums in individual schools is a first step. This will offer parents the opportunity to learn to exercise and reconcile their voices, and this may in turn lead to a reconfiguring of professional attitudes and assumptions on lay involvement in education. Somewhat ironically, such radical change may proceed from the discussion of apparently mundane issues connected to school life.

- However, the difficulties and complexities of engaging with and extending parental voice cannot be overlooked, and in most sites, any change is likely to proceed slowly and incrementally, and remain fragile and partial.

Note
1 Public (state) schools of choice appear to have no effect on increasing parent participation in activities or meetings (as compared to traditional state schools), but they do provide a statistically and substantively significant boost to parents' hours spent volunteering. Private secular schools appear, all else being equal, to decrease parental attendance at meetings and activities while there is some evidence that they increase the amount of volunteer time by a magnitude similar to public schools of choice. The most interesting results are found for the case of private religious schools. Here the results suggest that after controlling for the observable covariates and accounting for selection on unobservables, these schools markedly decrease the participation of parents (as measured in both attendance at events and meetings and hours spent volunteering) relative to those in traditional public schools (Buckley 2007).

6 Capability and capacity: remodelling the workforce

Frank Coffield

6.1 The government's approach

Capability and capacity make up the final element of the PMSU reform model, where 'capability' refers to the skills and abilities of the workforce and 'capacity' to the infrastructure of institutions.[1] The government's approach, which will be explained before any criticism is offered, is to move the public services from central control to continuous self-improvement, and it acknowledges that such a transformation needs to secure the engagement of public service professionals:

> Staff must be brought into the process, because as the deliverers of any change, their engagement is essential to successful implementation. Studies show that staff feel change is being well-managed when their views are being listened to and when reasons for change are well-communicated.
>
> (PMSU 2006a: 86)

At a number of points throughout the PMSU report, the same argument is repeated, reinforced and extended. For example:

> Research shows that if staff are dissatisfied so too are customers … front-line staff are often the first to know when a policy is not working and when users are displeased. Engaging staff in the change process is also essential because they are potentially key advocates of public service reform.
>
> (ibid.: 78)

We mentioned in Chapter 1 that the document also recognises the limitations of top-down performance management, while claiming at the same time that these limitations can be successfully addressed.

To improve the 'calibre, skills, attitude and motivation' (ibid.: 11) of the workforce, the government has introduced a range of measures which can be summarised under three headings:

- Investment in 'inspirational' leadership, e.g. the National College for School Leadership and the Centre for Excellence in Leadership for the post-16 sector: 'There is evidence of a strong correlation between effective leadership and organisational performance' (ibid.: 82).

- Reform of the workforce by creating new roles (e.g. teaching assistants), performance-related pay, faster career progression and greater recognition (e.g. teaching awards).

- By 'capturing', 'showcasing' and 'championing' (ibid.: 83) best practice, and by offering incentives for different types of partnerships.

If anything, the government's policy review, entitled *Building on Progress: Public Services*, published in March 2007, presents this message more forcibly by, for example, introducing the chapter on the workforce with this pledge: 'The Government must harness the commitment, dedication and skills of public service workers' (HMG 2007: 55). It then goes further by recommending four ways in which the government 'must listen better to staff and involve them in planning' (ibid.: 59):

- by reducing the number of top-down controls and devolving more decision-making;

- by encouraging Ministers and senior civil servants to 'shadow' front-line staff;

- by giving staff the chance to develop ideas proactively in partnership with policy-makers;

- by giving staff stronger roles in setting targets.

We also wish to acknowledge the government's efforts to create a well-qualified workforce and we will use improvements in the post-compulsory sector to illustrate their plans. In the White Paper on Further Education (DfES 2006) the government announced support for the development of the workforce, which has for many years been seriously neglected. Since then, eleven Centres for Excellence in initial teacher training have been established throughout the country; a mandatory requirement of 30 hours of continuing professional development a year for tutors in post is to be introduced; and all newly appointed college principals will be expected to achieve a qualification in leadership within three years of being selected. These are substantial and welcome investments.

Before turning to our critique, we also want to record the considerable common ground that exists between the government and ourselves. First and foremost, we are agreed that the beneficiaries of all these investments, new buildings and professional endeavour are the students and not the teachers. So our main aim is the same as that of the government, namely, to improve the quality of the education system *in the interests of all learners*, a phrase we prefer to 'capacity building' or 'workforce development'. We deliberately say *the interests* of all learners and not their wishes, because at times the wishes or demands of a minority of learners conflict with the best interests of the majority, and at other times it is the other way round. Moreover, we agree that no learner should have to put up with poor teaching, and in what follows there is no suggestion that the professionals always know best. There will always be tensions between the need for professional autonomy and the need for regulation to deal with poor performance. Where we part company from the government is our conviction, based on research evidence, that their model of change will not produce the outcomes which we all desire.

6.2 Critique

We are being invited to accept that we are on the cusp of a new, more radical, and apparently more progressive, phase of reform; it is therefore an ideal time to take stock. First, this policy review is clearly a response to the repeated failure of previous administrations (both Conservative and New Labour) to win over the professionals working in the public services. Second, this new model of change is advice offered from the centralising administration of Tony Blair to his successor, Gordon Brown, and it was not a plan which it would itself be called upon to implement. In this respect the government was acting rather like St Augustine, who wished to be chaste – but not quite yet. Third, the new model of reform represents such a complete volte-face from a government which has for ten years been so wedded to central command and control that we are entitled to ask: Will this government, will any government, be prepared to let go, to transfer some power to the professionals?

There are, moreover, some further and perhaps more serious concerns with the new model of reform. By constantly emphasising the need for the workforce to be more flexible and responsive to users, the impression is created that the professionals are the main obstacle to progress rather than the main means of achieving that progress. Highlighting the need to remodel the workforce means that other critical factors are ignored such as long-standing and major inequalities in levels of funding between, for example, further education and the school sector, or between adult education and further education – inequalities which sustain staff resentment rather than commitment. The substantially increasing investment in all the public services since 1997 is acknowledged, but that followed eighteen years of neglect; and, despite increased investment, under-funding continues to plague many key services. And it is not only levels of spending which are ignored in these two documents; so too are governance and the institutional architecture, both of which have an impact on the quality of services.

Furthermore, there is a disjuncture between the model and the arguments used to support it. In the model the views of the staff do not appear; it is the voice of users which is privileged. All the right words are used – in the modern jargon 'all the right buttons are pushed' – but there is no mention of the most obvious and appropriate mechanism, namely, the introduction of systemic feedback loops whereby staff could become involved in the evaluation, formation and redesign of policy. In short, the model in PMSU is not nearly as progressive as the text.

Matthew Taylor, one of the architects of the policy review, *Building on Progress*, has pointed to 'the gap between the framework and day-to-day practice' (2007). That gap is more like a gulf, because neither document betrays any understanding of the difficulties in bringing about lasting change. For example, the discussion paper from the PM's Strategy Unit argues: 'If staff do not understand or believe the rationale for change, they are unlikely to be able to advocate it' (2006a: 78). Agreed, but staff are being asked to do much more than understand the rationale for change. As Michael Fullan has been pointing out for years, 'change has to *occur in practice*' (1991: 37, original emphasis); and that involves the multidimensional use of new materials, new teaching approaches and a fundamental alteration in the beliefs, assumptions and theories of tutors. No wonder so little real change takes place.

It is difficult to resist the conclusion that, despite all the official rhetoric of harnessing the commitment of public sector workers, staff are being invited to buy into a model of reform which has already been decided upon centrally. The government appears to see its task as one of engaging public sector professionals in the local delivery of centrally formulated plans. This conclusion is supported by the occasions when the progressive mask slips to reveal a worrying slide to authoritarianism. For instance, the PMSU document reveals how the new Service Transformation Board of officials will 'challenge inconsistency or deviation from agreed standards or best practice' (2006a: 85). This statement reveals no appreciation of the complexities involved in deciding not only what is to count as 'best practice', but also in working through all the stages needed to disseminate it (on which topic, see Coffield and

Edward, forthcoming). But worse is to follow: once standards have been agreed and best practice 'captured' (by whom? using what criteria?), no deviation is to be allowed. What has happened to all the promises of 'giving staff the chance to develop ideas proactively, in partnership with policy-makers?' (HMG 2007: 59).

Further evidence for the view that central control will not be easily relinquished comes from an interview with Michael Barber, who moved from being head of the Standards and Effectiveness Unit in the DfES to lead the PM's Delivery Unit, which then applied the principles of school reform to the rest of the public services. The interview is quoted approvingly by the PMSU document. When asked what lessons could be learned from education reform in England, he replied that school inspection should be used 'to check that people were adopting better practices ... you need to design mechanisms to make sure that the program is faithfully implemented' (Barber 2006. 3–4). The concern is not that the government wants to steer policy in a particular direction; the worry is that it also wants to dictate which rowing stroke should be used.

The PMSU paper, as quoted earlier, claims: 'There is evidence of a strong correlation between effective leadership and organisational performance' and it cites two studies (Muijs *et al.* 2004 and Thomas 1988) in support. That claim both simplifies and exaggerates the complex findings of these detailed research studies. For instance, Muijs *et al.* argue that different leadership styles are required at different periods in the evolution of an institution; and that recently there has been a move away from inspirational heads towards 'a realisation that the most effective means for true improvement lies in more distributed and democratic forms of leadership, involving teachers in leading their schools' (2004: 156).

6.3 An inappropriate model of leadership

There are also problems with the government's model of leadership which is broken down into a number of expectations and specifica-tions, each of which is divided further into underpinning components. The example given here is from Further Education (FE), but the same approach has been adopted for school leadership. As part of the government's plan to professionalise the workforce in FE, the Skills Council for the post-compulsory education and training sector (LLUK), issued for the first time in November 2006 the role specifications for newly appointed and serving principals. These specifications will 'underpin the development of the Centre for Excellence in Leadership's new qualifying programme for FE principals ... will help college boards of governors to recruit and appoint principals ... and assist in the performance review and professional development of existing and aspiring principals' (LLUK 2006: 3). They have also 'been subjected to comprehensive national consultation' (ibid.).

The plan consists of 11 role expectations and six broad specifications which are broken down into

- 54 activities

- 46 areas of knowledge, and

- 92 personal and professional qualities.

That makes in total 11 role expectations and 192 role specifications, one of which (K 5.5) is sub-divided into a further 13 sub-sections. Together they present such a formidable battery of essential activities, knowledge and qualities, that is very likely to make even the Archangel Gabriel think twice about submitting an application. George Miller in a famous psychological article entitled 'The magical number seven, plus or minus two' pointed out in 1956 that the average memory span for most adults is seven items, with some individuals managing to deal with nine and others with only five. This finding holds good for lists and for larger chunks of information – but who can cope with 203?

Despite page upon page of detailed specifications, it is important to record what is missing from the LLUK's list. There is no mention anywhere of a definition of learning or theories of learning and how they could be used to improve the quality of teaching and learning by students, tutors, principals and FE colleges.

The specifications could be summed up as the qualities needed to implement government reforms faithfully and to monitor the new practices required of staff to meet centrally determined objectives and targets. Ironically, the 203 requirements are handed down from on high as part of the sector's move to 'self-regulation'.

6.4 Implications for policy

- We need to expand the role of teachers as innovative and responsible professionals, who would still remain accountable for their practices. This could be achieved in part by providing discursive space for professional growth and local initiatives. As Wallace and Hoyle argued,

  within broad limits of acceptable practice, teachers' discretion is essential for educational improvement because of their need to adapt to contingent and relatively ambiguous circumstances. Policy makers have apparently failed to comprehend the nature of professional practice.

  (2005: 10)

- A rigorous system of dealing with poor performance by institutions or tutors will continue to be needed, although the problem is not as great as all the tough talk by government ministers would have us believe.

- Forums should be provided to bring together staff from different tiers of the system (e.g. national, regional, institutional leaders, middle managers and front-line staff) to meet to discuss the strengths and weaknesses of policy initiatives, how they are being mediated, interpreted and enacted. This is similar to the suggestion in *Building on*

Progress that 'panels of public service workers should be used more methodically, giving staff the chance to develop ideas proactively, in partnership with policy-makers' (HMG 2007: 59). Such forums could be the beginnings of systematic feedback loops which any self-improving system will need.

- Each sector within education requires strong, financially stable institutions which retain sufficient discretion to plan their immediate, short-term and long-term futures. Providers within an area should also be held jointly responsible for local levels of participation and achievement (see Stanton and Fletcher 2006).

- We need a different model of leadership from the heroic, transformational approach espoused by government, which implies that there is a simple, causal relationship between leadership and organisational performance. We need to move to a more distributed, post-transformational model, which disperses power to colleagues, parents and students, which facilitates collective learning and where social interactions are based on mutual trust (see Collinson and Collinson 2005).

- Our alternative approach will seek to strike a better balance between central direction and local discretion; and between the current hectic pace of change and the need of institutions for stability and of students for continuity and order.

- We need to become more humble, less ambitious and more realistic about the prospects of rapid, large-scale 'transformational' reform driven from the centre. Over the last ten years we have learned not only about 'the law of unintended consequences … for every policy initiative there will be unpredicted and unpredictable results' (Fink 2003, quoted by Wallace and Hoyle 2005). We have also seen the harm done by the law of perverse but foreseeable consequences, which could have been prevented if only professionals had been consulted earlier.

- Finally, David Miliband in his speech on the public services, at the launch of the PMSU document, made much of the themes of renewing the spirit of democracy, of empowering citizens, and of power 'being devolved to the lowest appropriate level' (2006: 3). One group is consistently omitted from his list of possible beneficiaries – professionals in the public services, whose knowledge and expertise are needed to further the interests of the main beneficiaries, the learners.

Note
1 This is the explanation offered at a seminar in October 2006 by Wendy Pyatt who led the team which prepared the PMSU document.

7 Improving the quality of the education system

Frank Coffield

7.1 Introduction

Let us begin by restating our basic position. We welcome the improved performance of the education system since 1997 which is visible, for instance, in the marked reductions in the numbers of failing schools and local authorities. Investment has also increased significantly over the same period: funding per pupil has doubled, as has the number of support staff, and there are now 36,000 more teachers than ten years ago (PMSU 2006b). We are also in agreement with the basic aim of the government to improve still further the quality of the education service. We conclude, however, that, based on our reading of the research evidence in education, the new reform model will be unable to realise that aim.

In this chapter we shall first recap briefly our main concerns with the top-down performance management used since 1997 and with the new reform model, both of which have been explained in detail in Chapters 3 to 6. We also want to account for our decision not to suggest an alternative model of our own. We then describe three problems which help to explain why radical and enduring change is so difficult in education. Finally, we outline three general principles which we consider to be essential to systemic reform in education.

7.2 The story so far

The examination of literacy policy in Chapter 3 pointed out that neither the original nor the revised targets have been met and that, after some initial successes, the literacy and numeracy strategies have shown a much more modest influence on outcomes. Bob Linn reviewed the use of tests in 50 years of educational reform in the US and concluded that 'the pattern of early gains followed by a levelling off is typical' (2000: 6). Another difficulty was that the pace of innovation being driven by the centre outstripped the capacity of schools to make lasting change. In the language of David Tyack and Larry Cuban (1995) the reforms were exceeding any sensible pedagogical speed limit. Indeed innovation was being valued over and above consistency and quality; and the proliferation of policy encouraged superficial rather than deep improvements. In contrast to the claims of the PMSU that 'other countries are following similar approaches' (2006b: 6), Gemma Moss argued that we could learn much from practice in Scotland, where some of the same levers are used but in a very different way, where pedagogy remains more a matter of professional judgement, and where the most power is not given to those who know little about professional practice. Scotland has been able to avoid, for example, the unwarranted imposition from the centre of one method of reading (synthetic phonics), a decision for which there is no adequate research evidence. Scotland is not being used by us as a model of excellence, far less perfection – like everyone else the Scots are struggling with improving performance across the system as a whole – but as an example of where there appears to be a better balance between change and continuity and between the powers of policy-makers and professionals.

In the fourth chapter, on market incentives in schools, Rebecca Allen and Anna Vignoles reviewed a very extensive literature in this country, the US, Sweden, and New Zealand and came to rather different conclusions from those arrived at by the Strategy Unit. As far as the UK is concerned, no causal connections have been established between, on the one hand, choice and competition and, on the other, student attainment. This is partly because choice and competition are limited. Only a small minority of parents (around 20%) have benefited so far from the right to choose. There are also limitations to the application of market principles in education. For the principles to operate fully, for example, schools must be able to expand, contract and shut down – but very few do so. It is true that school choice has not worsened socio-economic segregation across schools as yet, although with school rolls falling and the potential for choice increasing, great care will need to be taken to limit selection by schools to prevent greater segregation.

Clearly the genie of school choice is out of the bottle and here to stay, but it is also clear that school choice has not proved a panacea to raising standards of student attainment. Equally, we acknowledge that if school choice were to be abolished, educational segregation across schools would not be massively reduced as it reflects social segregation in housing. Rather than abolishing school choice we need better safe-guards against selection of students by schools to prevent unacknowl-edged and implicit selection by, for example, socio-economic background and ability which may be brought about under the cover of formal selection criteria that are allowed within the terms of the admissions code, such as the degree of someone's overt religiosity. Where schools are oversubscribed, government may need to consider other mechanisms to determine admissions, such as lotteries.

Carol Vincent in Chapter 5, after reviewing the evidence, concluded that the versions of choice and voice presented by PMSU are not strong mechanisms for reform in education. While voice may have greater potential as a lever of change, the government discussion document does not recognise the difficulties in fostering an individual or a collec-tive voice for parents. These include: defensiveness from teachers, reluc-tance from parents, and the expression of illiberal or competing voices. Moreover, not all parents possess the same social, cultural and material resources to exercise voice. The potential of voice, however, lies in establishing small, local forums, where parents are provided with the opportunity to exercise and reconcile their voices, on legitimate matters of concern, and where a genuine consensus between parents and teachers can be achieved. Change, however, is likely to be slow and incremental and to remain fragile and partial. It is also not clear how differences between voices can be reconciled.

The fourth and final feature of the reform model is concerned with improving the capacity of the workforce. After ten years of top-down performance management, the government is acutely aware that it must now harness the commitment of the professionals, and it has made substantial and welcome investments in all levels of the workforce from initial training through in-service training to leadership. If staff are to be treated as essential partners in the process of reform, however, the government will have to share power with the professionals by, for example, creating feedback loops which enable professionals to explain the strengths and weaknesses of policy in practice and to be engaged in redesigning policy. Frank Coffield raised the question whether a government which has been so committed to top-down performance management can itself learn to change its approach so radically and form more equitable relationships with the professionals. The change to a new administration under Gordon Brown at least provides the opportunity for such a conversion.

The model of leadership espoused by government will also have to change because the current version is focused on faithfully carrying out whatever reforms the government stipulates. We need a more open and democratic model of leadership; and training which can equip leaders to recognise their central responsibility for improving the quality of learning and to dedicate the appropriate time, space and resources to build teacher learning communities.

In sum, we have examined in some detail each of the four main elements in the government's reform model and we have not found them nearly as effective or powerful as the Strategy Unit would have us believe. The outcomes from top-down performance management have become modest after initial success. No causal connection has been established between school choice and student attainment. Parental voice has not yet proved to be a strong lever of change; and the government has only very belatedly recognised the need to engage the good will and creativity of the teaching profession. The model also assumes that the different kinds of pressure it places on the workforce can be easily assimilated. It does not attempt to describe how differences between these pressure points and what they seek from the workforce will be reconciled.

7.3 An alternative model?

When we had reached this point in our discussion, we considered that our next task was to produce an alternative to the neat, elegant and seductively simple model proposed by the PMSU. As an icon, it appears to possess both economy (it holds a lot of disparate ideas together) and power (it suggests the government strategy for reform has an interactive structure and an implicit hierarchy). These appearances are, however, deceptive. Basically, the model is a response to the problems that policy-makers now face after ten years of overusing one mechanism of change – namely, top-down management – which has alienated the professionals; it is not a response to the problems faced by practitioners. The model appears to be a coherent whole, but, as we have seen, the research evidence for it is weak, mixed or non-existent. In short, it is a patchwork of disparate elements which are frequently in conflict with each other and which hide the real tensions in the system by pursuing a variety of different mechanisms at one and the same time, thus sending out confusing messages. A simple model has been arrived at by the expedient of understating all the difficulties and complexities inherent in each of its four main elements. We do not wish to be seduced by simplicity nor to be captured by the managerialist language: the world of professional practice and the task of improving it on a national scale are much more complicated and messier than this model, or any model, would suggest. We therefore decided not to suggest an alternative model of our own.

7.4 Three problems

Instead we propose different ways of conceptualising the problems now facing public sector reform, and we suggest different principles of procedure. Any principles, however, for improving the quality of learning throughout the educational system must begin by acknowledging the full complexities of that task. We shall discuss three.

(i) Layers of complexity

First, improving the quality of learning on a national scale is not a technical problem which can be solved by pulling the appropriate 'levers' or applying sufficient pressure. Systemic reform must grapple with extensive local variation in provision and multiple layers of complexity within each local setting. The view from the centre strips out the complexity of local conditions and simplifies in order to justify decisive action. But professional practice means dealing precisely with high levels of complexity and finding ways to handle them without distortion. To take the example of sixth forms, the DfES explains how 'provision varies dramatically between areas where there is no school sixth form provision at all, and areas where every school has a sixth form' (2004: 70). It includes a chart with seven categories of sixth form provision from 0% to 100%, and this complicated chart simplifies the variability by excluding sixth form colleges and tertiary colleges.

Any process of educational reform must also take account of the following layers of complexity:

- the content and status of the subjects being taught, the syllabus, and the impact of a high-stakes assessment regime on teaching;

- the different pedagogy thought appropriate to teach each of these subjects;

- the organisational structures and management arrangements

in institutions and the governance of the sector as a whole;

- the abilities and dispositions of the students and how they vary in different settings;

- the abilities, professional experience and dispositions of the teachers and the quality of their relationships with students;

- the historical and geographical locations of institutions which have created a bewildering variety of unequal school systems and schools, reflecting deeply rooted social and economic inequalities;

- the different resources at the disposal of particular institutions, including the physical infrastructure, different kinds of engagement with local communities, and access to relevant support and expertise beyond the institution;

- the level of technology and its relevance to the particular pedagogical task in hand;

- the impact of national policies on funding, planning, inspection, initiatives and qualifications;

- socio-economic and cultural influences on education generally and on the purposes of education in particular.

These factors not only interact with each other. More importantly the patterns of interaction differ in the tens of thousands of classrooms up and down the country. As Marnie Thompson and Dylan Wiliam argue,

> Learning – at least the learning that is the focus of the formal educational enterprise – does not take place in schools. It takes place in classrooms, as a result of the daily, minute-to-minute interactions that take place between teachers and students and the subjects they study.
>
> (2007: 1)

(ii) The grammar of schooling

Tyack and Cuban (1995) employ an historical perspective in trying to understand why, in the US, for over a hundred years schools have changed reforms rather than reforms changing schools. This brings us to the second difficulty in enacting new policy in schools: what they call 'the grammar of schooling'. Just as grammar organises meaning in verbal communications so, they argue, 'the basic grammar of schooling, like the shape of classrooms, has remained remarkably stable over the decades' (1995: 85). By this arresting phrase they mean such organisational regularities as the division of knowledge into different subjects, the private world of teachers isolated in a classroom with students, and the age grading of students, all of which shape the ways in which teachers work. In other words, plans for reform need 'a sophisticated understanding of the school as an institution [and] insight into the culture of teachers' (1995: 113). It is exactly that type of understanding and insight which is missing from the PMSU document.

(iii) A 'self-improving' system?

There is a third important issue we wish to introduce to the debate before turning to our own principles of reform, namely, a more comprehensive notion than exists in the Strategy Unit's document about what it means to move towards a 'self-improving' system. The phrase is repeated frequently within the text, but it is nowhere fleshed out apart from the remark that 'This model is described as self-improving because it seeks to embed incentives for continuous improvement and innovation within the system' (2006a: 21).

Cynthia Coburn's work is helpful here in suggesting how we need to move beyond counting minimal improvements in test scores, or in the number of schools adopting a particular reform, to creating deep and lasting change. She proposed that there are four interrelated dimensions to scaling up reforms in order to create a 'self-improving' system:

- depth – 'change that goes beyond surface features ... to alter teachers' beliefs ... and underlying pedagogical principles' (2003: 4);
- sustainability – change which is continued over time, after the initial enthusiasm and resources have dissipated;
- spread of reform principles from classrooms to school policies and to the system itself;
- a shift in the ownership of reform so that it becomes an internal rather than an external reform with authority for it held by local authorities, schools and teachers, 'who have the capacity to sustain, spread and deepen reform principles themselves' (2003: 7).

Taken together, these four elements of scaling up reforms call for nothing less than deep, cultural and sustained change which will take years of hard, patient work to implement. They also require steady management and partnerships between all the main players that can only be developed over the long term. This brings us to the first of our three principles.

7.5 Three principles for improving the quality of learning

(i) A more moderate pace of change

First, as a nation we need to give up the macho talk of 'quantum leaps', 'step changes' and 'transformational change' in education. Such phrases are attractive to politicians who have to work to a four-year electoral cycle and an annual cycle of public spending reviews and so are understandably keen on quick results to appease the electorate and the media. But it makes no sense to those engaged in the slow, painstaking job of improving professional practice. The timescales of politicians and professionals are at variance, and that brute fact needs to be incorporated into the planning of new policies, which cannot just be 'rolled out' like carpets. To argue as Tony Blair, Gordon Brown and Ruth Kelly did in the foreword to the White Paper on Further Education that 'evolutionary and incremental change will not be enough' (DfES 2006: 2) only reveals that politicians do not understand the problems involved in reforming professional practice. Schools also need to keep the twin pressures for development and maintenance in a healthy balance. As David Hargreaves and David Hopkins put it,

> Schools need some continuity with their present and past practices,
> partly to provide the stability which is the foundation of new
> developments and partly because the reforms do not by any means
> change everything that schools now do.
>
> (1991: 17)

Given the complexities of the existing system and the difficulties in achieving lasting change, we need to adopt a more humble approach towards reform. As Mike Wallace and Eric Hoyle argue, once it is accepted that 'tightly controlled transformational reform is unrealistic, a more promising alternative becomes promoting incremental improvement within broad consensual limits of acceptable practice' (2005: 1). We shall return to their final point about the 'limits of acceptable practice' at the end of this chapter.

(ii) More equal power relations

We need nothing less than a new settlement between central government and the teaching profession, with less central control and regulation and more involvement of teachers in the formation, evaluation and redesign of policy as full, active partners. In other European countries educational policy is formed and reformed more slowly through social partnerships, based on the democratic participation of all the key players. The teachers' unions are trusted and respected members of these democratic partnerships and have joint ownership of any changes proposed. The reforms which Sir Michael Lyons has recently suggested for local government should also be applied to education, for instance, 'the importance of changed behaviours in all tiers of government, of local flexibility, and the pressing need to inspire a sense of powerfulness' in the teaching profession (2007: ii).

A recurrent theme in the earlier chapters has been the need for a more equal sharing of power, not just between politicians and policy-makers on the one hand, and professionals on the other, but also between teachers and parents and between teachers and students. It is, however, the unusual politician, policy-maker or professional who voluntarily relinquishes power. It is also a reasonable proposition that teachers, namely those who have the most first-hand experience of schools and who are held accountable for the success or failure of their institutions, should be involved in policy formation, implementation, evaluation and redesign. In the words of Tyack and Cuban, teachers need to be 'enlisted in defining problems and devising solutions adapted to their own varied circumstances and local knowledge' (1995: 137). Our reading of the PMSU document suggests that the high point of centralisation has probably passed, but easy talk of decentralisation has still to be turned into changed behaviour on the part of ministers.

The claims made above for teachers to be given more responsibility can, with equal merit, be advanced for parents and students. In Chapter 5, Carol Vincent has made a strong case for the establish-ment of parental forums in schools, which may 'lead to a reconfig-uring of professional attitudes and assumptions on lay involvement in education'. Similarly, Gert Biesta and David James (forthcoming) argue that one of the main drivers for improving learning is for tutors and managers to maximise the opportunities for students to contribute to their own learning. Again, such a move calls for a shift in the power relations between professionals and students towards joint collaboration.

There remains the issue of how much flexibility should be given to practitioners so that they can adapt any particular reform to their local circumstances. In this regard it is worth drawing on the experience of one of the most promising interventions in education, namely, the movement in favour of assessment *for* learning rather than assessment *of* learning, which takes the professional development of teachers as its central axis of efforts to build capacity. After years of careful experimentation in both the UK and the US, Thompson and Wiliam came to the conclusion that interventions need to be both tight and loose. As they explained:

> The 'Tight but Loose' formulation combines an obsessive adherence to central design principles (the 'tight' part) with accommodations to the needs, resources, constraints, and particularities that occur in any school or district (the 'loose' part), *but only where these do not conflict with the theory of action of the intervention.*
>
> (2007: 48, original emphasis)

By the 'theory of action of the intervention' they mean its core principles. So the main message appears to be that power needs to be shared with practitioners to accommodate local conditions, but that such flexibility must be within the limits imposed by the core principles of the intervention. This change programme uses the creative tension between never telling teachers which techniques they should employ in their classrooms and holding them accountable for the decisions they make.

(iii) Teaching and learning at the heart of the system

Our third and final principle is also the most important. If the aim is to improve the quality of learning throughout the education system, then most attention should focus on the key relationship which makes that happen, namely, that between tutor and students in thousands of classrooms up and down the country. The core business of education is teaching and learning. These are best seen not as two separate activities but as the two sides of one coin, a joint endeavour whose aim is to enable students to achieve the maximum of which they are capable. The research evidence points unequivocally to the development of teacher professionals as 'the fundamental lever for improving student learning' (Thompson and Wiliam 2007: 2); teacher expertise can also be developed slowly through teacher learning communities (for further details of how these communities work in practice, see Black *et al.* 2003; Borko 2004; Watkins 2005) and 'this takes time and structures that support extended, systematic, reflective practice' (Thompson and Wiliam 2007: 25). There are clear resource implications to these proposals which should become the urgent concern of policy. The intention is to shift deliberately the attention of head teachers, principals, senior management teams and teachers away from meeting targets, responding to initiatives and maximising funding to placing teaching and learning at the centre of their professional lives, through sustained, collaborative learning with colleagues. Indeed, we would go so far as to say that, once the quality of teaching and learning begins slowly to improve, then success in meeting all the other objectives is more likely to be achieved. Current practice appears to be predicated on the opposite notion, namely, that if schools and colleges are run as efficiently and effectively as private businesses, then the quality of learning will somehow improve as a by-product. Schools and colleges are first and foremost centres of learning and only secondarily, if at all, businesses.

There is one final, thorny topic which we must address and which we mentioned in the Introduction: can we afford to leave reform to the professionals? Will it be sufficient to develop their expertise and creativity? Can we trust all 400,000+ teachers in this country to behave altruistically in the best interests of their students? On the one hand, we reject the simplistic division, based on the work of Julian Le Grand (2006), of professionals into knights or knaves and of institutions into 'beacon schools', 'coasting colleges' and 'failing schools'. On the other hand, we are acutely aware of the time and effort some teachers spend on such useless innovations as brain gym, fish oils and learning styles (see Coffield *et al.* 2004). We conclude that, while the professional empowerment of teachers is a necessary condition of success, it is not in itself a sufficient condition. We need new and more equal partnerships between practitioners, academic researchers and policy-makers, working towards goals which are clearly shared with parents and students. We take our stand with Wallace and Hoyle, who argue for 'expanding the scope for teachers to serve education as responsible and creative professionals, while monitoring that their practices lie within the limits of acceptability' (2005: 5). Nowadays, we are all accountable.

Taken together, our three principles call for an end to the excesses of the target-driven, punitively accountable and initiative-led programme of reform to which education has been subjected over the last ten years. Instead, we argue for a more modest but more realistic programme, which would seek to strike a more harmonious and productive balance between reform and maintenance, between a more moderate pace of change and sustainability; between central direction and local flexibility to accommodate varying conditions, between 'light' and 'loose'; and between teacher empowerment and professional accountability, with teaching and learning at the heart of the system.

References

Adler, M. and Raab, G. (1988) 'Exit, choice and loyalty: the impact of parental choice on admissions to secondary schools in Edinburgh and Dundee'. *Journal of Education Policy* 3(2): 155–179.

Ahlin, A. (2003) 'Does school competition matter? Effects of a large-scale school choice reform on student performance'. Uppsala University discussion paper.

Allen, R. (2007a) 'Allocating pupils to their nearest secondary school: the consequences for social and ability stratification'. *Urban Studies* 44(4): 751–770.

— (2007b) The effect of school competition on pupil performance: a review of literature. Institute of Education: mimeo.

Allen, R. and Vignoles, A. (Nov 2007, forthcoming) 'What should an index of school segregation measure?' *Oxford Review of Education* 33(5).

Arend, N. and Lent, A. (2004) *Making Choices*. London: New Local Government Network.

Armstrong, F. (2003) 'Difference, discourse and democracy: the making and breaking of policy in the market place'. *International Journal of Inclusive Education* 7(3): 241–257.

Ball, S. J. (2003) 'The teacher's soul and the terrors of performativity'. *Journal of Education Policy* 18(2): 215–228.

— (2007) *Education plc: Understanding Private Sector Participation In Public Sector Education*. London: Routledge.

Barber, M. (2006) Education reform lessons from England. Online: www.educationsector.org/analysis/analysis_show.htm?doc_id=344385.

Bayer, P. and McMillan, R. (2005) *Choice and Competition in Local Education Markets*, NBER WP 11802. Cambridge, MA: NBER.

Belfield, C. R. and Levin, H. (2003) 'The effects of competition on educational outcomes: a review of US evidence'. *Review of Educational Research* 72(2).

Benhabib, S. (1996) 'Towards a deliberative model of democratic legitimacy'. In S. Benhabib (ed.) *Democracy and Difference*. Princeton, NJ: Princeton University Press.

Besley, T. and Ghatak, M. (2003) 'Incentives, choice, and accountability in the provision of public services'. *Oxford Review of Economic Policy* 19: 235–249.

Bettinger, E. P. (2005) 'The effect of charter schools on charter students and public schools'. *Economics of Education Review* 24: 135–147.

Biesta, G. and James, D. (forthcoming) *Improving Learning Cultures in Further Education*, London: Routledge.

Bjorklund, A., Edin, P.-A., Fredriksson, P. and Krueger, A. (2004) *Education, Equality And Efficiency: An analysis of Swedish school reforms during the 1990s*. Stockholm: IFAU.

Black, P., Harrison, C., Lee, C., Marshall, B. and Wiliam, D. (2003) *Assessment for Learning: Putting it into practice*. Maidenhead: Open University Press.

Black, S. E. (1999) 'Do better schools matter? Parental valuation of elementary education'. *Quarterly Journal of Economics* 114(2): 577–599.

Blair, T. (2006) 21st-Century Public Services speech, 6 June 2006. Online: http://www.number10.gov.uk/output/page9564.asp.

Booker, K., Gilpatric, S., Gronberg, T. and Jansen, D. (2005) 'The effect of charter schools on traditional public school students in Texas: are children who stay behind left behind?' Texas A&M University discussion paper.

Borko, H. (2004) 'Professional development and teacher learning: mapping the terrain'. *Educational Researcher* 33(8): 3–15.

Bradley, S., Johnes, G. and Millington, J. (2001) 'School choice, competition and the efficiency of secondary schools in England'. *European Journal of Operational Research* 135: 527–544.

Brodie, I. (2003) *The Involvement of Parents and Carers in Sure Start Local Evaluations*. London: National Evaluations of Sure Start (NESS).

Brown, P. (1998) 'The "third wave": education and the ideology of parentocracy'. In A. Halsey, H. Lauder and P. Brown (eds), *Education, Culture, Economy, Society*. Oxford: Oxford University Press.

Buckley, J. (2007) *Choosing Schools, Building Community: The Effect of School Choice on Parent Involvement*. Occasional paper no.133. National Centre for the Study of Privatisation in Education. Online: http://www.ncspe.org (accessed 22 May 2007).

Buddin, R. and Zimmer, R. W. (2005) 'Is Charter School competition in California improving the performance of traditional public schools?' RAND Education working paper.

Burgess, S. and Slater, H. (2006) *Using Boundary Changes to Estimate the Impact of School Competition on Test Scores*, CMPO discussion paper 06/158. Bristol: CMPO.

Burgess, S., McConnell, B., Propper, C. and Wilson, D. (2007) 'The impact of school choice on sorting by ability and socio-economic factors in English secondary education'. In L. Woessmann and P. Peterson (eds), *Schools and the Equal Opportunity Problem*. Cambridge, MA: MIT Press.

Clark, D. (2004) 'Politics, markets and schools: quasi-experimental evidence on the impact of autonomy and competition from a truly revolutionary UK reform'. Berkeley: University of California: mimeo.

Coburn, C. E. (2003) 'Rethinking scale: moving beyond numbers to deep and lasting change'. *Educational Researcher* 32(6): 3–12.

Coffield, F. and Edward, S. (forthcoming) 'Rolling out "good", "best" and "excellent" practice: what next? Perfect practice?' *British Journal of Education Research.*

Coffield, F., Moseley, D., Hall, E. and Ecclestone, K. (2004) *Should we be Using Learning Styles? What research has to say to practice*. London: Learning and Skills Research Centre.

Coldron, J. and Boulton, P. (1991) 'Happiness as a criterion of parental choice of school'. *Journal of Education Policy* 6(2): 169–178.

Collinson, C. and Collinson, D. (2005) *Leadership Challenges*. Lancaster University: CEL.

Crozier, G. (2000) *Parents and Schools*. Stoke: Trentham Press.

Cullen, J. B., Jacob, B. and Levitt, S. (2005) 'The impact of school choice on student outcomes: an analysis of the Chicago public schools'. *Journal of Public Economics* 89: 729–760.

Deem, R., Brehony, K. and Heath, S. (1995) *Active Citizenship and the Governing of Schools*. Buckingham: Open University Press.

Department for Education and Skills (2003) *Excellence and Enjoyment.* London: DfES.

— (2004) *Five Year Strategy for Children and Learners: Putting people at the heart of public services.* London: Stationery Office.

— (2005) *Higher Standards, Better Schools For All: More choice for parents and pupils.* London: Stationery Office, Cm 6677.

— (2006) *Further Education: Raising skills, improving life chances.* London: Stationery Office, Cm 6768.

Dixit, A. (2002) 'Incentives and organizations in the public sector'. *Journal of Human Resources* 37: 696–727.

Equalities Review (2007) *Fairness and Freedom: The final report of the Equalities Review*. Online: www.theequalitiesreview.org.uk.

Fine, M. (1997) '[Ap]parent involvement: reflections on parents, power and urban public schools'. In A. Halsey, H. Lauder, P. Brown and A. Stuart Wells (eds), *Education, Culture, Economy, Society.* Oxford: Oxford University Press.

Fullan, M. (1991) *The New Meaning of Educational Change*. London: Cassell.

Garmarnikow, E. and Green, A. (1999) 'The "Third Way" and social capital: Education Action Zones and a new agenda for education, parents and community'. *International Studies in Sociology of Education* 9(1): 3–22.

— (2007) 'Social capitalism and educational policy: democracy, professionalism and social justice under New Labour'. Paper presented at CfPS seminar series, March 2007, Institute of Education, University of London.

Gibbons, S. and Machin, S. (2006) 'Paying for primary schools: admissions constraints, school popularity or congestion?' *Economic Journal* 116: 510, C77–C92.

Gibbons, S., Machin, S. and Silva, O. (2005) Choice, Competition and Pupil Achievement. Discussion paper. Centre for Economics of Education, LSE.

Gillborn, D. and Youdell, D. (2000) *Rationing Education: Policy, practice, reform and equity*. Buckingham: Open University Press.

Gillies, V. (2007) *Marginalised Mothers*. London: Routledge.

Glass, N. (2005) 'Surely some mistake?' *Guardian* (*Society Guardian*), 5 January 2004, p.4.

Goldstein, H. and Noden, P. (2003) 'Modelling social segregation'. *Oxford Review of Education* 29: 225–237.

Gorard, S., Taylor, C. and Fitz, J. (2002) 'Does school choice lead to "spirals of decline"?' *Journal of Education Policy* 17(3): 367–384.

Greene, J. P. and Winters, M. A. (2004) 'Competition passes the test'. *Education Next,* Summer 2004.

Griffith, A. and Smith, D. (2005) *Mothering for Schooling.* London: RoutledgeFalmer.

Hargreaves, A. (1996) 'Revisiting voice'. *Educational Researcher* 25(1): 12–19.

Hargreaves, D. H. and Hopkins, D. (1991) *The Empowered School: The management and practice of development planning*. London: Cassell.

Harlen, W. and Deakin Crick, R. (2002) 'A systematic review of the impact of summative assessment and tests on students' motivation for learning'. London: Institute of Education. Online: http://eppi.ioe.ac.uk.

Hastings, J. S., Kane, T. J. and Steiger, D. O. (2005) *Parental Preferences and School Competition: Evidence from a public school choice program.* NBER WP 11805, Cambridge, MA: NBER.

Hatcher, R., Troyna, B. and Gewirtz, D. (1993) *Local Management of Schools and Racial Equality* (final report to the Commission for Racial Equality). London: CRE.

Hirschman, A. (1970) *Exit, Voice and Loyalty.* Cambridge, MA: Harvard University Press.

H M Government (2007) *Building on Progress: Public services.* London: Cabinet Office, Prime Minister's Strategy Unit.

HMIE (2002) *How Good is our School?* Online: http://www.hmie.gov.uk/hgios/hgios.asp.

Hoxby, C.M. (2000) 'Does competition among public schools benefit students and taxpayers?' *American Economic Review* 90(5): 1209–1238.

— (2003a) 'School choice and school competition: evidence from the United States'. *Swedish Economic Policy Review* 10: 9–66.

— (2003b) *The Economics of School Choice.* Chicago: Chicago University Press.

— (2005) *Competition among Public Schools: A reply to Rothstein*, NBER WP 11216. Cambridge, MA: NBER.

Johnston, R. and Watson, J. (2005) *A Seven Year Study of the Effects of Synthetic Phonics Teaching on Reading and Spelling Attainment.* Online: http://www.scotland.gov.uk/Publications/2005/02/20682/52383.

Krueger, A. B. and Zhu, P. (2004) 'Another look at the New York City School Voucher Experiment'. *American Behavioral Scientist* 47(5): 658–698.

Lareau, A. (1989) *Home Advantage: Social class and parental intervention in elementary education.* London: Falmer Press.

Le Grand, J. (2006) *Motivation, Agency and Public Policy: Of knights and knaves, pawns and queens.* Oxford: Oxford University Press.

Levačić, R. (2004) 'Competition and the performance of English secondary schools: further evidence'. *Education Economics* 12(2): 179–194.

LLUK (2006) *Benchmark Role Specifications for Principals of Further Education, Sixth Form and Specialist Colleges.* London: LLUK.

Linn, R. L. (2000) 'Assessments and accountability'. *Educational Researcher* 29(2): 4–16.

Luttrell, W. (1997) *Schoolsmart and Motherwise: Working class women's identity and schooling.* London: Routledge.

Lyons, M. (2007) *Place-shaping: A shared ambition for the future of local government.* London: Stationery Office.

Martin, J. (1999) 'Social justice, education policy and the role of parents: a question of choice or voice?' *Education and Social Justice* 1(2) 48–61.

Miliband, D. (2006) 'Public services and public goods: lessons for reform'. Speech, 6 June. Online: www.nationalschool.gov.uk/news_events/psrc2006/downloads/speech_david_miliband.pdf.

Miller, G.A. (1956) 'The magical number seven, plus or minus two: some limits on our capacity for processing information'. *Psychological Review* 63: 81–97.

Mouffe, C. (1993) *The Return of the Political*. London: Verso.

Muijs, D., Harris, A., Chapman, C., Stoll, L. and Russ, J. (2004) 'Improving schools in socioeconomically disadvantaged areas: a review of research evidence'. *School Effectiveness and School Improvement* 15(2): 149–175.

Newman, J. (2000) 'Beyond the New Public Management? Modernising public services'. In J. Clarke, S. Gewirtz and E. McLaughlin (eds) *New Managerialism, New Welfare?* London: Sage, pp. 45–61.

Noden, P. (2000) 'Rediscovering the impact of marketisation: dimensions of social segregation in England's secondary schools, 1994–1999'. *British Journal of Sociology of Education* 21(3): 371–390.

Ofsted (2002a) *The National Literacy Strategy: The first four years 1998–2002*. London: Ofsted.

—— (2002b) *The Curriculum in Successful Primary Schools*. London: Ofsted.

OISE (2003) *Watching and Learning 3*. London: DfES.

Phillips, A. (1999) *Which Equalities Matter?* Cambridge: Polity Press.

Power, M. (1994) *The Audit Explosion*. London: Demos.

Prime Minister's Strategy Unit (2006a) *The UK Government's Approach to Public Service Reform: A discussion paper*. London: Cabinet Office.

—— (2006b) *A Report on Schools: Progress in the last ten years and challenges ahead*. London: Cabinet Office (30 November).

Ranson, S., Arnott, A., Martin, J. and McKeown, P. (2003) *The Participation of Volunteer Citizens in the Governance of Education*. Final report to the ESRC.

Ranson S., Martin, J. and Vincent, C. (2004) '"Storming parents", schools and communicative action'. *British Journal of Sociology of Education* 25(3): 259–274.

Reay, D. (1998) *Class Work*. London: UCL Press.

Reay, D. and Wiliam, D. (1999) '"I'll be a nothing": structure, agency and the construction of identity through assessment'. *British Educational Research Journal* 25(3): 343–354.

Rothstein, J. (2005) 'Does competition among public schools benefit students and taxpayers? A comment on Hoxby (2000)'. NBER WP 11215, Cambridge, MA: NBER.

Rouse, C. E. (1998) 'Private school vouchers and student achievement: an evaluation of the Milwaukee parental choice program'. *Quarterly Journal of Economics* 113(2): 553–602.

Sandstrom, F. M. and Bergstrom, F. (2005) 'School vouchers in practice: competition will not hurt you'. *Journal of Public Economics* 89: 351–380.

Select Committee for Education and Skills (2005) *Fifth Report of Session 2004–05 (secondary education)* (Vol. Appendix I).

Stanton, G. and Fletcher, M. (2006) '14–19 institutional arrangements in England: research perspective on collaboration, competition and patterns of post-16 provision'. Nuffield Review of 14–19 Education and Training, Working Paper 38. Online: www.nuffield14–19review.org.uk.

Taylor, M. (2007) 'Demanding parents and staff with drive are keys to success'. *Times Educational Supplement*, 23 March.

Thomas, A. B. (1988) 'Does leadership make a difference to organizational performance?' *Administrative Science Quarterly* 33(3): 388–400.

Thompson, M. and Wiliam, D. (2007) 'Tight but loose: a conceptual framework for scaling up school reforms'. Paper presented at American Educational Research Association, Chicago, 9–13 April.

Torgerson, C., Brooks, G. and Hall, J. (2006) *A Systematic Review of the Research Literature on the Use of Phonics in the Teaching of Reading and Spelling.* London: DfES.

Tyack, D. and Cuban, L. (1995) *Tinkering Towards Utopia: A century of public school reform*. Cambridge, MA: Harvard University Press.

Vincent, C. (1992) 'Tolerating intolerance? Parental choice and race relations – the Cleveland case'. *Journal of Education Policy* 7(5): 429–443.

— (1996) *Parents and Teachers: Power and participation.* London: RoutledgeFalmer.

— (2000) *Including Parents.* Buckingham: Open University Press.

— (2001) 'Social class and parental agency'. *Journal of Education Policy* 16(4): 347–364.

Vincent, C. and Martin, J. (2002) 'Class, culture and agency'. *Discourse* 23(1): 109–128.

— (2005) 'Parents as citizens: making the case'. In G. Crozier and D. Reay (eds), *Activating Participation: Parents and teachers working towards partnership.* Stoke: Trentham Books.

Walkerdine, V. and Lucey, H. (1989) *Democracy in the Kitchen.* London: Virago.

Wallace, M. and Hoyle, E. (2005) 'Towards effective management of a reformed teaching profession'. Paper presented at a seminar of the Teaching and Learning Research Programme, King's College, London, 5 July.

Watkins, C. (2005) *Classrooms as Learning Communities: What's in it for schools?* London: Routledge.

West, A. and Pennell, H. (1999) 'School admissions: increasing equity, accountability and transparency'. *British Journal of Education Studies* 46:188–200.

West, A. and Varlaam, A. (1991) 'Choosing a secondary school: parents of junior school children'. *Educational Research* 33: 22–30.

West, A., Hind, A. and Pennell, H. (2004) 'School admissions and "selection" in comprehensive schools: policy and practice'. *Oxford Review of Education* 30(3): 347–369.

Williams, F. and Churchill, H. (2006) *Empowering Parents in Sure Start Local Programmes.* London: Sure Start.

Woods, P., Bagley, C. and Glatter, R. (1998) *School Choice and Competition.* London: Routledge.

The Work Foundation (2005) 'Think piece – contestability in the learning and skills sector'. Online: http://www.dfes.gov.uk/furthereducation/uploads/documents/contestability_think_piece_the_work_foundation.doc

The Bedford Way Papers Series

A full list of Bedford Way Papers, including earlier books in the series, may be found at www.ioe.ac.uk/publications